Strange Saga of Zack Tillerman

Book 3 of Wannasea Tales

NG Rippel

Copyright© 2024

All rights reserved.

ISBN: 978-1-917327-11-4

Contents

Next move 4
Wrinkles in time 8
Resolution 14
Hard slog 26
Coming down 34
Darkness Arrives 43
Unexpected Reunion 48
Solo 58
Restructuring 63
Unmoored 68
Big Time 75
Back to Iraq 83
A Different Course 88
Fine Tuning 96
Wedding Plans 101
Gone Flyin 106
The Journals 111
End Of Production 118
Moving On 124
Incidental Contact 129
Questions 135
Needs 141
Night Out 149
Tweed Conner 168
Losing Control 176
A Wedding 182

Unexpected Guest	189
Performances	199
Off To See The Wizard	205
Return Path	213
Mending Fences	222
The Calm	230
The Expected Unexpected	241
Respite	249
Familiar Sound	259
Exit Stage Left	269
Path To Nowhere	276
A Conundrum	294
Interment	299
Reunion	303

Next move

Wednesday, January 8, 7:02PM. Zack nods to Abe, as he turns toward the band to make certain that they are ready to perform. Abe rises from his chair, picks the wireless microphone up from the table, then heads to a position in front of the stage.

"Welcome ladies and gentlemen," Abe says into the microphone after switching it on. "Tonight, we shall have an evening of sea and other songs from Zack Tillerman and Company. You are encouraged to sing along to the stanzas. I sincerely hope that you will enjoy the performance."

Zack and the band break into 'The Place' which most of the audience seems to know. They sing along loudly and cheer when Zack follows the song up with 'Wannasea Pirates'. Toward the end of the second song, three young women come through the front entrance and go to the table where three empty seats had been reserved by another young woman.

Abe notices that Zack is now peering intently into the crowd. Zack repeats the last refrain of the song three times, each time moving closer to the front of the stage. When the last stanza is sung, rather than breaking into the next song, Zack sets down his guitar and says into the microphone, "I need to take a short break. I'll be right back. The band will play you some sea shanties until then."

The band appears to be as perplexed as the audience, but quickly recovers and begins playing "Roll the Old Chariot around". as Zack jumps from the stage and races toward the table where the three young women just sat down. As he does, a very tan, lanky young woman with quite striking features rises from the table and tries to make her way out of the front entrance. Zack catches her by the elbow three feet before the open doorway.

"It's time to stop running Abby," Zack says to the young woman. "You are not seventeen anymore. You don't have run away from what scares you."

"I'm not running," the young woman with the golden hair says. "I am trying to protect you, RJ."

"I am fully capable of protecting myself," Zack tells her.

"Zack," Molly calls out from her position at the front entrance, "you need to get back up on the stage!"

"I'll be back in a minute," Zack replies to Molly as he guides the young woman out the front door. "Tell my dad to play a few more sea songs until I return."

"What is it that are you trying to protect me from, Abby?" Zack asks as he leads the young woman to the left side of the entrance..

"Me," Abby says. "Seems I'm only capable of bringing you trouble."

"I'm fully capable of dealing with any trouble you may bring," Zack says.

Abby turns and grabs hold of both of Zack's arms and hugs him tightly as they come to a stop just off the entrance to 'The Place'.

"After I came out to see you play in that bar in Halifax," Abby tells Zack, "I felt certain that what we used to be was behind both of us. Then Cindy showed me one of your videos of your last few songs. Those songs told me that we need to talk but I couldn't figure out how to go about it."

"You have the ability to see me anytime that you want," Zack replies. "There's no law against it on this Island."

"There's the law of reason," Abby replies. "As you've said, I'm no longer 17."

"What stopped you from trying to see me after your parents shipped you off to Switzerland?" Zack asks. "What stopped you from trying to get in touch with me while I was in the Army? You knew where Saanvi and my mom lived. They would have put you in touch with me."

'I was in Leeds when you went into the Army," Abby replies still holding on to Zack tightly.

"They didn't have phones there?" Zack asks.

"It wasn't that simple, RJ," Abby says. "It's never been that simple."

"What's stood in the way of your seeing me," Zack says. "Your parents?"

"My parents likely would be unhappy knowing that I've come out here to see you, but at this point my parents have very little control over me. I live my own life. I've also lived enough to know that our lives seem headed in completely different directions. My problem is that I can't seem to move myself along without having some kind of closure with you."

"We choose those directions, Abby. I think at a minimum you owe me an explanation about what happened to you and our child."

"I can't right now," Abby says as she squeezes Zack even tighter.

"Will there be a time when you can?" Zack asks. Then says less earnestly, "Listen, I really need to get back in there."

"Can we do something on Friday morning if I come out here?" Abby asks.

"It's the same for me as it's always been, Abby," Zack says. "I will meet you wherever and whenever you want."

"10:30 at the ferry terminal on Friday morning?" Abby asks.

"Okay," Zack says as Abby releases her grip on him slightly.

"Give me your cell phone number," Abby says as she gradually moves away from Zack.

Zack pulls his smartphone from his back pocket and swipes to turn it on.

"The number is at the top," Zack says.

Abby pulls her phone out of her pocket and puts the number into a message which she sends to Zack with the entry: "contact info". Zack then takes his cellphone back and saves Abby's contact info. Abby has saved the number which Zack has given her under the heading "Cello instructor".

"Zack," Molly shouts from the front entrance of 'The Place', "You need to get back in here this instant!"

"I promise that I will come on Friday," Abby says before placing a kiss on Zack's cheek. "Please be there."

The pair slowly move back toward the front entrance. As Zack pulls open the door with his right hand, he realizes that Abby is sliding her hand out his left hand. Zack had not realized that he had been holding on to Abby's hand.

Before Zack, Abby proceeds into the dining area and immediately goes back to her table without turning around to look at Zack, who moves quickly onto the stage as the band is the final stanza of "Blow the man down".

"Sorry for the interruption, folks," Zack says into the microphone. "I had some urgent personal business which needed to be addressed. I promise that I will make it up to you."

Zack turns and whispers to the band, "Stuck in my mind".

Wrinkles in time

Thursday, January 9, 3:43 PM. Abe and Zack are seated at the audio control room portion of the recording area of the SouthTown studio. Just as they have for the past 3 weeks, Zack and Abe are alternatively working on lyrics related to Zack's memories of Iraq and exploring what lies behind them.

"Where were you when your father was killed?" Zack asks Abe, startling him with the directness of the question.

This is the first time in ages Abe can remember anyone asking him that particular question. At the time when the bomb in the trunk of his grandmother's car exploded, most everyone on Wannasea Island knew where Abe and his mother were. Abe had no memory of having provided anyone with an answer to this question previously.

"I was standing with my mother about a block and a half from where the ferry dock traffic circle is now," Abe says. "We were watching people enter the ferry for the first run over to the Mainland. I was a little upset that I wasn't allowed to go with them. About a minute earlier, I watched my grandmother and father cross the street, a block down from us. My dad had parked their car about two blocks up Mountain Way, so they would be able to get back up to the Government Center quickly after the ceremony. I was watching the passengers fill the ferry when the explosion went off. The sound echoed between buildings and shattered most of the window glass. I remember my mother grabbing onto my hand. I was 8 ½ years old then and didn't want my mother holding my hand, but as we moved toward the area where crying and screaming was originating, holding my mother's hand no longer bothered me. We went around the corner and I could see the fire from the explosion burning where my grandmother's car had been. The front of most of the buildings on Mountain Way had been blackened. The grocery store beside where my dad had parked had collapsed. There were people bleeding and lying in the streets. The Constabulary had been doing crowd control for the ferry dock opening, so they were on the scene almost immediately. Then the sirens started. We were only able to get within a block of where my grandmother's car had been. We got as close as we could and stood there looking to see if we could understand what had happened. I remember that almost everyone, who walked by us, said, "I am so sorry." My mother and I were paralyzed until the Captain of the Constabulary finally came and walked us home. We lived in a flat where the grocery store now sits down by the Medical Center. It has been over 63 years since that explosion happened, but I can step right back into it as if it were happening right now."

"That's exactly how I feel about the IED which killed Clint and Hi," Zack responds.

"I used to believe that incident had created its own separate reality," Abe says. "That the explosion existed by itself and could be called upon to become my reality at any time. It took me years to realize that explosion had embedded itself within me. The explosion took over a big portion of my being. The explosion is still here inside me."

"Same with me," Zack says. "When I think back to that day, I remember how still everything was. It gave me a spooky feeling. I can remember going out on at least a hundred such scouting expeditions with Clint and Hi. I'd never felt that stillness before. I was talking to them on the headset inside my helmet. Telling them how nothing was moving. Then I felt the explosion. Suddenly I was flying. I was in the air. I could feel my backside burning. I knew immediately that not only wasn't my life ever going to be the same, but that instant had been embedded in my soul."

"Do you remember hitting the ground?" Abe asks.

"No," Zack replies, "I just remember flying in the air. It felt as if I had been sent flying for the rest of eternity. I have no memory of landing. If I had been a little closer to the stream when the explosion went off, I would have landed in it and drowned. When I came to, there was another APV parked beside me and a Medic telling me to lie still. I remember feeling like I was burning up. Then I remember a helicopter coming and people moving me on a stretcher and into the helicopter. Then I was flying again. I've not really stopped that flying since."

Two members of 'The NorthEnders' come into the studio carrying their musical instruments.

"Let me go help get the guys set up," Zack says to Abe as he moves toward the live room.

Dave enters with the other NortherEnders.

For the next 90 minutes, Dave sits at the console with Abe off to the side as Zack and the band fine tune the first song which Abe and Zack have been able to create from Zack's Iraq memories.

Abe has not witnessed Zack being as fussy with any song before as he is with this one. Zack has an image in his head of what he wants this song to be and won't give up on fine tuning until it matches that image. Finally, Zack is satisfied, and Dave begins recording. After four takes, this is the result:

Chadwick and Williams *118 BPM in key of D Major in 12/8 time*

>not easy getting out of North Birmingham
>when you're caught in a legal jam
>with the mob on the wrong side of the equation
>getting out of town doesn't require much persuasion
>
>Clint and Hi became military men
>hoping never to run into the Johnson Crew again

didn't really know what they were doing
other than to war they'd soon be going

learned to pilot vehicles tracked and untracked
into dusty towns and through hell and back
they'd played that game for five long years
when I became their final set of eyes and ears

Chadwick and Williams
fast talking, slow walking desert pilgrims
Calm Clint and Headstrong Hiram
had the great fortune to get to know them
as we rumbled through Anbar and all its delirium
moving ever closer to our appointment with oblivion

started playing guitar in the shade of our CHU
Clint teaching me every single chord that he knew
Hiram commented, bitched, sang and chattered
asking me to play every song he felt mattered

just past Hit things didn't look right
the scene was too still, the air much too quiet
not even a roaming herd of goats could be spied
as I went off to find where dangerous things might hide

traveled forty meters down the side of the hill
nothing looked disturbed, the morning air remained still
Clint nudged the APV forward as a horrible crackle filled the air
everything flying through the orange haze in a lasting nightmare

Chadwick and Williams
fast talking, slow walking desert pilgrims
learned to pilot vehicles tracked and untracked
into dusty towns and to hell and back

> Calm Clint and Headstrong Hiram
> had the good fortune to get to know them
> as we rumbled through Anbar and all its delirium
> moving ever closer to our appointment with oblivion
>
> knocked face first to the hard Iraqi ground
> fifteen minutes before I came around
> Chadwick and Williams were gone
> like it or not, life always goes on
>
> Chadwick and Williams
> fast talking, slow walking desert pilgrims
> learned to pilot vehicles tracked and untracked
> into dusty towns and to hell and back
>
> Calm Clint and Headstrong Hiram
> had the good fortune to get to know them
> as we rumbled through Anbar and all its delirium
> moving ever closer to our appointment with oblivion
>
> through Anbar and past delirium
> arriving at the appointment with oblivion
> Chadwick and Williams now gone
> like it or not, life always goes on
> like it or not, we still live on
>
> like it or not, this life goes on
> through Anbar and past delirium
> arriving at the appointment with oblivion
> like it or not, we still live on

Zack puts down his electric guitar and walks out of the live room. He crosses behind where Dave and Abe sit.

"Now comes the hard part," Zack says, "figuring out what we are going to do with that song."

"What kind of music is that song?" Dave asks.

"Stuck in Iraq blues," Zack replies.

"I'm not sure that's a thing," Abe says.

"Let's see if we can make it one," Zack replies.

Resolution

Friday, January 10, 10:31AM. Zack is standing just outside the exit of the ferry dock. Abby is walking toward him dressed in an orange halter top, bright white shorts and sandals. Abby gives Zack a broad smile. Zack does his best to hide his surprise that Abby has actually shown up.

"How was the trip over?" Zack asks.

"Beautiful," Abby replies. "Couldn't ask for a better day to be out on the water."

"Do you want to grab a coffee of something?"

"Why don't we go walk on a beach somewhere?" Abby suggests.

"Let's go out to Southwest Beach," Zack replies. "It's usually kind of quiet out there."

Zack guides Abby down the block to the parking lot where his battered VW Beetle is parked.

"RJ," Abby says as she climbs into the dented vehicle, "you really need to get rid of this thing. It's an eyesore."

"Only to people, who do not appreciate its history,' Zack replies with a slight edge to his voice. "Sorry," Abby said, "I didn't realize you had a personal attachment to this vehicle."

"I'm averse to throwing away things which are still serviceable," RJ responds. "This thing gets me where I want to go."

"What happened to it?" Zack spends the next five minutes explaining the blaster ball attack at Beth's house.

"I didn't think those kinds of things happened out here," Abby says after Zack has finished his explanation.

By this time, they had turned on to West Road on their way around the mountain.

"You promised that you'd tell me what happened to you when they sent you away," Zack says.

Abby places her hand atop Zack's left hand which is on the gear shift.

"My mother took me to Tocino, Switzerland, where I had an abortion on the third day," Abby says softly. "After a week of recovery, I was shipped to a boarding school in Montreux, where I spent the next 8 months. When I finished there, for the next 4 years I was at the university in Leeds. The past year and a half, I have been finishing my education at the conservatory in Coventry."

"Wasn't there any way for you to try to contact me from any of those places?" Zack asks as he turns on South Mountain Way.

"At the boarding school in Montreux, absolutely not. I was not allowed to have a telephone or use a telephone. The school held my passport. I tried writing postal letters but after 6 months, I realized the letters were being thrown away. When I got to Leeds, I did manage to get in touch with Cindy. She told me she heard that you had gone in the Army and were in Iraq. At that point, I thought it would be best if I stayed out of your life. Did you try to get in touch with me?"

"Non-stop for six months," Zack replies. "None of your friends would talk to me. Either in person or by phone. For most of those 6 months, I was also dealing with the trouble which your family was making for my parents and me."
"Trouble?" Abby says taken aback, "What possible trouble could my family have created for you?"

"They had me kicked out of the Conservatory," Zack replies. "I had to go back to North Halifax to finish my secondary education. Hanover University made it clear that I was "persona non grata". They saw to it that my father was fired from his job at the docks. He had to do piece work away from our district for two years to get by. They had my mother fired from her job in the Hanover Court system."

"How do you know my parents did this?" Abby asks.

"Both at the Conservatory and North Halifax, it was made clear to me that because I had offended your family, I no longer belonged there " Zack replies. "The company which fired my father told him that instructions for his firing had come from your father's company. In my mother's case, no one would confirm anything, but it seems relatively clear that your father had some role in seeing that my mum was dismissed as well."

"I'm having difficulty believing this," Abby says.

"Abby," Zack says as he swings right on South Road, "you can believe whatever you want. All I am telling you is what I know. Your father is a very powerful man. The main reason that I went in the Army was in hope that your father would stop blackballing my father from being able to work around Halifax."

The car goes silent for two minutes until they reach the parking lot for Southwest beach. The lot is about half full.

"I'm really sorry RJ," Abby says squeezing Zack's hand. "I had no idea that is how things turned out for you and your family."

"It's water under the bridge," Zack says as he swings into a parking spot in the second row and turns off the engine.

"Before we go for out walk there is something else which you really have to know," Abby says. "I'm engaged to be married in June after I finish up at the conservatory."

This news does not surprise Zack all that much. That this news doesn't immediately paralyze him is the true revelation.

As they walk toward the beach, Abby says, "That time I came over to see you play in the bar in Halifax is the day after Alex asked me to marry him. I still hadn't told him "Yes" when I came to the bar."

"Why did coming to the bar have anything to do with your response?" Zack asks as he begins walking the beach in an easterly direction.

"I had to know that you were all right," Abby replies. "Cindy told me that she heard you were playing at some dive. I thought if I saw you performing, I could move on with my life."

"Did it?" Zack asks as he places his hands in the pockets of his shorts.

"Seeing you playing at that bar made my heart ache," Abby says. "I could see that you seemed all right physically. I wanted so much to talk to you but felt if I did that all I would do is bring more harm than good."

"I would have really liked to talk to you then," Zack says softly.

"I don't think I could have done it," Abby says earnestly.

They walk along in silence for a long minute.

"You have certainly learned how to play guitar," Abby says to break the silence. "I couldn't tell it when I saw you in that bar, though. The music you were playing was pretty much garbage. You were performing it like you felt it was garbage too."

"It was," Zack says, "but it was all that Dave, the owner, would let me play. The people who came to that place, went there to drink not to listen to anyone play anything. No matter what the music might be. My primary job was actually being the bouncer. By the time you saw me, I'd learned my role."

"The music and that bar were pretty awful," Abby says with a grimace as she walks toward the incoming waves. "A few months later, I couldn't believe it when Cindy told me that you had become something of an internet sensation."

"So having become some kind of sensation is why you started having an interest in me again?" Zack asks.

"Absolutely not, RJ," Abby replies offended. "Originally, hearing your songs and seeing your videos meant that I could not keep pretending that you no longer exist or that I didn't care about you. I thought perhaps it wouldn't hurt if I simply became a fan of yours. Like some of my girlfriends."

Zack stops and stares directly into Abby's green eyes.

"That's rubbish," Zack says. "After what we went through seven years ago, you lost any ability to ever be just one of my fans. You know as well as I do that most of the last songs which I've released are about us."

"I wasn't absolutely certain of that," Abby replies sheepishly.

"Then you aren't really listening to what I am singing," Zack says looking away.

Abby begins walking through the foam of the waves which have just broken.

"Tell me about being in Iraq," Abby says.

"It was hot," Zack says testily. "It was dusty. It was dangerous. That's about it."

"Cindy said that you got wounded rather badly," Abby says.

"Not as badly as others," Zack says, returning to looking directly into Abby's eyes.

They walk silently for the better part of 100 yards before Abby returns from the edge of the foam and falls into stride beside Zack. She puts her hand on Zack's back and begins to gently rub it. She can feel the scar tissue.

Zack stops. Abby stops with him. Zack turns away from Abby and lifts the rear portion of his 'The Place' t-shirt to reveal the angry red welts on the lower portion of his back which continue down into his shorts.

"When they brought me back to Hanover," Zack says as he allows the shirt to drop back into place, "the running joke was that I had gotten my ass shot off in Iraq. The reality is that is a rather accurate description of what happened."

"Will you tell me about it?" Abby asks.

"No," Zack says firmly.

They walk silently for another fifty yards before Abby says softly, "I have no intention of hurting you or causing you any further pain. All I am trying to do is figure out how I still feel about you. I am at the point in my life where if I don't figure that out, it may create even bigger problems."

"You do realize," Zack says, "that I've have a choice in this matter as well?"

"I do, RJ," Abby says as she links her arm through Zack's left elbow and moves closer to his side. "Right now, my mind is telling me that it is absolutely insane to give any thought to trying to rekindle what we used to have. The problem is that my heart is telling me something entirely different."

"I'm not sure I'm ready to deal with that," Zack says as they continue down the beach.

"I'm starting to get a little thirsty," Abby says, "is there somewhere around here that we can get something to drink?"

"My trailer is right up the hill," Zack says. "If you want, we can go up there. I've got water and soda."

Abby hesitates for a moment before saying, "Okay but I have got to be out at Island Resorts by 2:30 to meet some of the girls from Coventry."

"It's a three-minute walk up to my trailer," Zack says as he turns to go back toward the parking lot, "I can drop you off at the Resort as soon as we have had something to drink."

"When did you learn to play guitar?" Abby asks as Zack guides her on a cross-corner course to the roadway which leads up to his trailer.

"In Iraq," Zack replies. "One of the guys there taught me the basics. After I started getting into it, I downloaded lessons from the web and spent most of my time practicing. In Iraq, I had plenty of spare time on my hands. By the time that I returned to Hanover, I was passable. I've been working on improving ever since."

"Those songs you did about alcohol," Abby says, "did you write them from first-hand experience?"

For the rest of the walk to the trailer Zack explains how he came to produce songs with Abe, as well as Abe's and his own grandfather's history of alcohol abuse."

"You didn't get into alcohol or drugs?" Abby asked as they reach the deck of Zack\s trailer.

"Music pretty much has always been my drug of choice," Zack says as he leads Abby to the patio table and chairs. "What do you want me to bring you?"

"Let me come with you and I'll choose," Abby says following Zack as he enters the front door of the trailer.

Abby follows him to the kitchen area.

"This place is really cute," Abby says, "and surprisingly clean." "I have cleaning people come in three times a week," Zack says. "They were just here this morning. Otherwise, it probably would be a mess."

"What would you like?" Zack says opening his refrigerator to reveal a selection of sodas, flavored and bottled waters.

"Just a regular water," Abby says as she walks back to the front living area to the where Zack has the cases for his musical instruments stacked against the wall.

"You still play the cello?"

"Once in a great while," Zack says as he hands Abby a bottle of water. He has grapefruit flavored water in his other hand for himself.

"Do you still have a violin?" Abby asks.

"In my room," Zack replies.

"Which one of those cases holds your cello?" Abby asks.

Zack points to the larger case toward the back of the living room. Abby walks to it and picks it up.

"Why don't you go get the violin and bring it out to the deck," Abby says as she carries the case out the front door.

Zack disappears into his bedroom and brings down the fiddle from the top shelf of his closet. He carries it out to the patio where Abby is in a chair by the table.

"Let me have the violin," Abby requests.

Zack hands it over to her.

"Get out your cello," Abby instructs.

Zack sits down at the chair on the other side of the patio table after pulling the cello and bow from its case.

Abby has begun adjusting Zack's fiddle.

"This thing is out of tune," Abby says as she adjusts the tuning pegs.

"It's tuned for sea songs," Zack replies.

"Let's do the Brahms double concerto," Abby suggests to Zack as she fiddles around playing the first bar.

They play for the next five minutes, getting progressively better before Abby signals to stop. There is no question that Abby is the better player of the two.

"Switch," Abby says as she rises and takes the violin from Zack.

She takes the cello from Zack and returns to her chair. They spend five more minutes playing Brahms' second concerto. Abby is now better on the cello than Zack had ever been.

"Where did you learn to play the cello like that?" Zack asks.

"At Coventry," Abby says. "Now let's switch back, I want to play 'Faded'."

"I'm not sure I remember it," Zack says.

Abby pulls out her cell phone and brings up the sheet music to Alan Walker's 'Faded'. They play the song through twice.

"That really wasn't too bad," Abby says. "If this Zack Tillerman thing of yours goes south, you might be able to make it with your cello."

Abby begins playing Zack and Abe's 'Stuck in my Mind'. At the second bar, Zack joins in on the cello. They are both smiling as they go through the song a second time.

"Hold that note," Zack says as he puts the cello back into the case and heads back into the trailer. "I will be back in a second."

Zack returns with his acoustic guitar.

"From the top," Zack says.

They perform the song once. Zack begins singing the words half-way through.

Zack stops playing and says, "Sing with me."

"I can't sing," Abby replies sheepishly.

Zack remembers now that Abby had avoided singing when they were in school together.

Thinking perhaps this was due to a lack of confidence, as Zack returns to playing guitar, he says, "Humor me."

Abby sings two verses with him before stopping and saying with a chagrined smile, "I told you I can't sing."

The two verses remind Zack that Abby\s voice was made for casting verbal spells on people, not singing.

When the song is ended, Zack begins playing 'carried away'.

"I'm not sure I know that one," Abby says.

Zack brings the sheet music up on his cellphone and puts it in from of her.

The pair spend the next hour playing a variety of Zack and Abe's songs. The end up by playing sea songs. The final song being 'Shant deceive her'.

"I really have to get out to the resort," Abby says looking at her watch which says 2:42.

Abby helps Zack take the instruments back into the trailer.

As they walk down the hill toward the parking lot and Zack's car, Abby asks, "Have you had any steady girl friends since you came back from Iraq?"

"I dated a nurse over in Hanover for about three months when I first got back," Zack replies. "It fell apart when she discovered that I really didn't have a plan for where I was headed."

Zack doesn't include that relationship had basically fallen apart when the nurse realized that Zack was not going to be getting over Abby any time soon.

Abby gives Zack a quizzical look.

"You weren't working toward the success which you now have?" Abby asks.

Zack shakes his head, "I kind of fell into it."

"You didn't fall into anything," Abby says earnestly. "You've been a good musician since I first met you. It just took you some time to figure out how to show it to the rest of the world."

"Did you have any other boyfriends before this guy you are engaged to?" Zack asks.

"No," Abby says. "I pretty much stayed away from relationships until after I finished at the university. I certainly wasn't looking to start anything when I met Alex."

"But now you are engaged."
"Now I am engaged," Abby says with uncertainly.

They walk in silence the rest of the way to Zack's car. In four minutes, Zack drives the short distance to Island Resorts.

"Just leave me at the front gate," Abby says. "That's where I am going to meet the girls."
Zack pulls his battered Bug off to the side before the entrance gates.

Abby leans over and kisses Zack on the cheek.

"Please don't try to get in touch with me," Abby says. "I may never contact you again. If I don't, know that I care for you and wish you nothing but the very best. Forget about me. Make the best of your talents. Know that I will be thinking about you and rooting for you from a distance."

As Abby moves to exit his car, Zack gently grabs Abby's elbow.

"About five months into being in Iraq," Zack says. "I finally figured out that I could get by without you. I loved you but I could get on with my life. Maybe it's better if we don't look back."

Tears come to Abby's eyes as she swings herself out of Zack's car. As Zack drives through the U-turn area before the Island Resort front gate, the guard at the station says to Abby as she walks by him.

"Isn't that Zack Tillerman?"

Abby smiles weakly and says, "Yes, it is."

Hard slog

Wednesday, January 15, 9:58AM. Zack parks his battered WV Beetle alongside Abe's Volvo at the SouthTown recording studio. As Zack exits his VW, Abe and Molly climb out of the Volvo.

Zack is somewhat surprised to see Molly. She has only been out to the studio one other time since it opened.

"Good morning partners," Zack says as he pulls his keys out of his pocket to open the side entrance to the studio. "What's the occasion?"

"We need to review our finances and distribute funds," Molly says. "Abe was headed out here, so I asked if I could ride with him."

"I'm just following orders," Abe says as they enter inside then pass through a small storage area and into the control room which is empty.

Zack switches on the lights as he recalls having promised Molly that he would do this task yesterday.

"I'm sorry I didn't come over yesterday," Zack says. "After I went down to the school to vote, I completely forgot about it. It took me forty minutes to get through the line. It was worth it though, just heard on the radio that the referendum passed."

A referendum to modify the island's aging legal code had taken place yesterday. The referendum required that at least 60% of voters approve of the proposed changes.

"Beth said that over 70% voted for it," Abe says as Zack pulls up another chair to the audio console.

"That result should make Olivia and Beth very happy," Zack says. Then pointing to the chairs in front of the console says, "Let's sit here."

The three sat themselves in front of the console.

"Those two put a lot of work into getting that referendum passed," Abe says. "Hopefully, the changes to voting registration will cause a lot more people living on this island to apply for citizenship."

"I know that I will," Molly says as she reaches into her briefcase and pulls out a stack of papers.

Molly finds the printouts which contain the current financials for ZackTillerman LLC. She hands one copy each to Abe and Zack.

"Based strictly on income," Molly begins, "the LLC did not do too bad last month. We took in almost $40k. We spent a little over $5K. That leaves us with $34,688 which can be distributed. Take a look and let me know if you have any questions."

Zack glances through the three-page printout. More to satisfy Molly than actually studying any of the information.

"Sales of seas songs are falling off," Molly says, "but the good news is that your live streams are more popular than ever."

"Do you think having 'The Shell' open had any impact on these numbers?" Abe asks.

"Probably," Molly says, "but we will need to wait a few months to figure that out."

"There is something which I am getting a little concerned about," Molly says looking at Zack, "I haven't received any bills from Dave for the recordings which you have had done here."

"I'm not sure we are planning on billing you for those recordings," Zack says. "It would kind of be me billing myself."

Molly rolls her eyes before saying, "No Zack. It would be whatever this business is called, billing ZackTillerman LLC.

You are part of both businesses but there are other people involved. You should be billing for those services."

"I'll talk to Dave about it," Zack says somewhat disinterestedly.

"I would also like to propose that we set a fixed schedule for having these meetings," Molly says. "Abe says we can use one of the conference rooms over at the new meeting center which is set to open next Sunday. I propose that we meet the second Monday of every month. What time is good for you two?"

"I'm always available," Abe says, "so whatever time is good for you."

"I go over to Hanover one Monday each month, " Zack replies, "to meet with Doc Schiller but I can arrange that schedule so it doesn't fall on second Mondays."

"How about 10AM?" Molly suggests.

Abe and Zack nod their heads in agreement.

"We need to keep in mind," Abe says, "that as part of our original agreement, after 18 months, any of us has the right to pull out of the LLC. In March, we will have reached the 18 month mark and will need to either amend our agreement or break things apart."
"I will note it, " Molly says, "and make certain that we deal with it at our meeting in February."

Molly pulls out another printout of the checking account for ZackTillerman LLC. She passes copies of the two-page document to Abe and Zack.

"This is our checking account and balance as of yesterday," Molly says. "I've left the balance at $10,000 which is the original amount which Abe put into the LLC. Look through it and let me know if you have any questions on any expenditures."

Molly waits a few minutes as Abe and Zack look over the printout.

Molly pulls out three checks which are the profit distributions for the partnership and a pen. She hands Zack his checks before sliding the other two checks on the console in front of Zack.

"You need to countersign our checks," Molly says.

Zack folds his check and places it in the inside pocket of his jacket behind his cellphone. He takes the pen which Molly is offering and scrawls his name in appropriate signature block of the other two checks.

"Abe says that you guys are working on producing some songs which you want to be treated separately on our website," Molly says. "Is there anything which I need to do?"

"These songs are different enough," Zack says, "that we need to figure out how they should be marketed before we put them up on the website."

"Different how?" Molly asks.

"The lyrics came out of my time in Iraq," Zack says. "I don't think that they can be used over at 'The Place' until we know if there is an audience for them."

"Isn't that pretty much what you did with 'This side of nowhere'?" Abe asks.

"I think 'This side of nowhere' fits into the other blues songs which we had at the time," Zack replies. "These Iraq songs are sort of off by themselves."

"Why don't we have a separate section in our sales area set up to try them out?" Molly asks. "How many of those songs do you have at the moment?"

"There is only 1 song which has been recorded so far," Zack answers. "I've got another one which I finished up last night which I want to try out on Abe this morning."

"What is your thinking of calling these types of songs?" Molly asks.

"I've been thinking of calling it "The Big Suck Blues"," Zack replies.

"Why that name?" Abe asks.

"'The Big Suck' is what we called our time in Iraq," Zack explains.

"I'd think about another name for it. I'd also suggest waiting to put any of the recordings for sale on the website until you have at least four or five of them finished," Abe says. "Until then, we can work on trying to figure out a way to market them."

"I'm more at the point of still wondering if we should market them at all," Zack says.

"What does Dave say?" Molly asks.

"He's only heard the first song," Zack says. "He thinks it's okay, but feels it needs to be tied into other songs to really go anywhere."

"That's pretty much my thought too," Abe says.

"Can I hear this first song that's been recorded?" Molly asks.

Zack switches on the audio console and finds the digital master of "Chadwick and Williams". He plays it back.

"You are right that it is different," Molly says. "I'm certainly no expert but I don't quite know what to make of it. Can I hear it again?"

"Sure," Zack says as he plays the recording again.

"It's certainly not catchy," Molly says, "but it does kind of reach out and grab you. Are you sure this is the kind of thing that you want to get into right now?"

Zack grimaces, "I don't think I've got any choice. When it comes to working on music, for whatever reason these 'Big Suck Blues' are all that I can wrap my head around now. I spoke with Doc Schiller about it last week. He suggested that I go with it. Unfortunately, it is taking me much more time to come up with these songs than it has to do everything else which we have done."

'Why don't you play the other song that you have ready?" Abe suggests.

"Okay," Zack says. "Come on in the studio with me."

The trio rise from their chairs and go into the live room. Zack pulls his electric guitar from the rear wall as Abe and Molly sit on the stools usually occupied by the other musicians. Zack spends a few minutes getting his guitar tuned, before he starts.

Hard Slog *105BPM in key of G Major in 4/4 Time*

long hard slog
no fit place for woman, man or wild dog
searching out the local demagogue
jumping through hoops playing military leapfrog
like crawling through an endless bog
another day of a long hard slog

when there is nothing to believe
no one except myself to deceive
it all comes down to
what none may undo
bodies scattered and lives wrecked
death will come when we least expect

there's no time to rest
does little good to protest
need to keep on keeping on
until the time comes to be gone
one more day spent in wartime fog
another day in a long hard slog

when there is nothing left to believe
and no one except myself to deceive
it all comes down to
what none may undo
bodies scattered and lives wrecked
death will come when we least expect

mind full of far-off dreams
trying to avoid explosive schemes
hidden in the culvert of dried up stream
matters not how loud we scream
we're only one tooth on the military cog
doing one more day of a long hard slog

when there is nothing left to believe
and no one except myself to deceive
it all comes down to
what none may undo
bodies scattered and lives wrecked
death will come when we least expect

like crawling through an endless bog
sounds become lost in combat's backlog
doing one more day of a long hard slog
one more day spent in wartime fog

like crawling through an endless bog
another day of a long hard slog
another day in a long hard slog
one more day in a long hard slog

Coming down

Saturday, January 18, 10:12PM. Zack has just completed his final set of the evening at "The Shell". He had done 'Don't blame it on the alcohol' twice but the audience is still clapping and calling out for him. Zack doesn't feel up to going back out on the stage as has been his usual practice for the past two months. Zack feels the beginning of the quick slide into the darkness.

Zack sits down on a plastic chair which someone has brought into the staging area. He's hoping what he's feeling is just the start of a cold but knows from the history of his last five years, those hopes are misplaced. He sits silently for a full five minutes as the band packs up.

"We're gone down to Sully's to get a sip," Jerome for 'The Northenders' says to Zack as the band begin to file out, "care to join us?"

"Thanks J," Zack says with a weak smile, "but I'm drained right now. Next time?"

Jerome nods his head and disappears down the side stairs with his bandmates.

Molly, who has been standing on the other side of the exit since the performance ended, says to Zack, "You might be a little less drained if you'd cut these performances down to 90 minutes like you promised."

"Not tonight, Moll," Zack says to Molly pleadingly, "I'm just not up to it."

Molly walks over to where Zack is sitting and puts her hand on Zack's forehead.

"Your forehead does feel a little warm," Molly says, "maybe you are coming down with something. Why don't you come over to my place and let me fix you something which will make you feel better?"

Normally such an offer from Molly would be cause for Zack to reject it out of hand, but tonight is different. Zack knows that as soon as he is alone, he is going to begin slipping into the realm of Chadwick and Williams. He will begin hearing Clint and Hi talking to him. If he drifts off to sleep, he is going to be right back in 'the Big Suck'.

Molly begins putting Zack's guitars in their cases after she locks the exit to the stage.

Zack rises slowly from the chair and places his electric guitar in its case.

"Let's just leave the guitar cases here," Zack says. "I'll pick them up on my way out."

"You're actually coming over to my place?" Molly asks, half in disbelief.

"I am," Zack says with a weak smile. "I'm counting on you to be able to fix me up."

"I'll do my best," Molly says as she takes Zack's arm and walks out the exit.

"You always do," Zack says, uncertain if he is talking to Molly or just himself.

Molly closes the staging area door and makes sure it is locked before walking with Zack around the seating area and to the rear entrance of 'The Shell'. It has begun to drizzle.

"I'm glad this rain didn't come earlier," Molly says as they move past people who are still clustered around the gate.

Zack tries to smile and wave back to the people, who are pointing and waving at him. Molly keeps Zack on course and through what little is left of the old patio area. They make their way to the driveway which leads up to 'Mountain Village' aka 'Tiny House Town'.

"They are really making progress on the Aquatic Center," Molly comments as they walk up the driveway past that area.

"Makes Abe happy," Zack says. "He comes up here to check on it every day."

"Do you think Abe is slowing down?" Molly asks.

"Abe seems pretty much the same as when I first met him a couple of years ago," Zack says. "Only difference is that he's got a lot more on his plate. He's going to start giving talks on those journals of his grandmother's the first of next month. I'm not sure I could juggle the buildout of the Center, songwriting, and planning talks about the journals."

"Fair point," Molly says. "He also spends a lot of time with the Twins."

They enter the parking area, then take a sharp left to go behind the laundry/restroom/shower area for the tiny houses. Molly is now renting the first 'double' just behind the laundry facility.

This is the first time that Zack has been to any of the tiny houses in the village.

"Do you like living here?" Zack asks.

'It's okay," Molly says. "I'm not planning on staying here forever, but for right now it is super convenient."

They walk across the deck in front of Molly's unit. Both the outside and inside lights switch on automatically when they walk past the sensor on the deck. Molly enters the code into the pad on the sliding door.

"Let me have your jacket," Molly says as they go inside.

Molly's unit has 400 square feet of living space with a small living room area in the front, a kitchen area complete with built-in in kitchen nook followed by a small built-in convertible couch which sits under the loft area where Molly sleeps. Molly has spent a good deal of time accessorizing her unit.

"Fancy," Zack says as Molly hangs his jacket up on hooks on the other side of the kitchen cabinet.

"I've become a fancy girl," Molly says with a big smile.

She leads Zack back to the built-in couch and picks up the tv remote. She switches the system, which is mounted to the rear wall of the kitchen area, on before turning it over to Zack. Zack hits the guide button and changes the channel to WWIN, the local island station which is now doing the nightly news. Zack lowers the volume to a whisper and sinks into the corner of the couch.

Molly pulls a forehead thermometer from the center kitchen drawer, goes to Zack, and presses it against his forehead.

"A little over 99," Molly says. "Maybe you have caught a bug?"

Molly returns the thermometer to the drawer and begins heating water in an electric kettle as she pulls out two mugs. She fishes into pantry for two packets of mint tea, honey, and a bottle of Jameson's whiskey which she sets on the counter next to the mugs. Molly then pulls out the right-hand drawer under the kitchen nook and retrieves a thick, green tartan throw. She takes the throw to where Zack is sitting and places it over him. She sits down next to him waiting for the water to boil.

"They are still talking about the referendum," Zack says to Molly.

"What else is there really to talk about on this island right now?" Molly comments. "Nothing will be going on with

Ainsley's trial until at least May. The casino doesn't open for another 6 weeks."

"Guess I don't watch tv much," Zack observes.

"How is Saanvi's wedding planning coming?" Molly asks.

"She has convinced my mom to stop thinking about inviting a cast of thousands," Zack responds. "The wedding is going to be inside 'The Place'. Mom has even agreed to let Sam & Sallie cater it. Mom is now dealing with a 100-person limit. Ray says that he'll have a hard time filling up the 35 people, who he is supposed to invite."

"Do you like Ray?"

"I do." Zack replies. "He's kind of had a rough life, but he's made the best of it."

"Rough life in what way?"

"He was raised by his grandmother," Zack explains. "His mother died when he was five. He worked in a grocery store up until he finally could make it as a free-lance journalist."

"Are Saanvi and Ray going to live on the island after they are married?" Molly asks as the kettle whistles.

"They are looking to buy a little place on the west side not far from my grandma's house."

Molly rises and goes to the kitchen where she begins preparing tea. She pours a good two shots of whiskey into Zack's mug and a single into her own. She brings Zack's mug and spoon over to him and sets it on the small side table.

"Let it steep for about 3 minutes," Molly advises.

The cellphone in Zack's jacket pocket buzzes loudly.

"I'd better get it," Zack says moving to rise from the couch.

"I'll get it for you," Molly says rising and moving to where Zack's jacket is hanging. She fishes in the pocket and pulls out his cellphone along with the check for over $20,000 which she had given him on Wednesday.

Molly returns to the couch, hands the cellphone to Zack.

"It's Marie," Zack says. "I forgot that I promised to stop up at the house to settle up for the week after the show."

"Do you need to go down there now?" Molly asks.

"I texted her back that I will come by tomorrow."

Molly rises and places Zack's check on the other side of the couch. She then returns to Zack's mug and extracts the teabag, stirring it with the spoon. She takes the spoon into the kitchen, where she does the same with her own mug of tea before returning with it to the couch. She lifts the throw and sets herself down as close to Zack as possible before reaching over with her right hand and picking up the check and presenting it to Zack.

"I forgot to take it to the bank," Zack says sheepishly as he takes the check and places it on the side table.

"Zack," Molly says, "you are one hot mess."

Zack picks up his tea and takes a big sip.

"Hey, this is pretty good."

"You are still a hot mess," Molly says before sipping on her own tea.

"I just can't seem to remember to do anything these past few weeks but work on these new songs."

"If you would let me," Molly says. "I'd be more than happy to take care of these kinds of things for you. I can see your checks get into the bank. I can see that you are settled up with Marie. I can see that your taxes are paid. I wouldn't even charge you anything for doing it because I like to do things for you."

Zack takes another big sip of his tea as he thinks, 'This is the problem with Molly'.

"You know that isn't right," Zack tells Molly. "That's a lot of work. You shouldn't be doing it for nothing."

Molly puts her tea mug into her right hand and takes Zack's hand with her left hand.

"I like to do things for you, Zack."

Normally at this point, Zack would break free. He'd take another sip of his tea, rise from the couch, thank Molly, and say good night. Tonight, he cannot bring himself to do it. He wants to remain sitting on the couch next to Molly. He doesn't even mind that Molly is now holding his hand.

"I'll let you do it," Zack finally says, "if you will let me pay you for it. How much will it cost?" Molly thinks for a moment, smiles then says, "$200 a month."

"That's ridiculous," Zack says, "I'll pay you $400 a month, or I'll keep doing it myself."

"You mean, keep not doing it for yourself," Molly says.

"$400 a month."

"Deal," Molly says leaning over and kissing Zack on the cheek.

Molly wiggles herself even closer to Zack. Molly is warm. Right now, Zack needs warmth.

Zack continues to sip on his tea as the news on the tv ends. The programming switches to a late-night talk show.

"You know that you could be on one of those shows if you want," Molly comments.

"What would I do on a talk show other than make a fool of myself?"

"There are people, other than just myself, who would like to hear you talk about your life," Molly says. "What causes you to play and produce the music that you do. Where you learned to play. They'd probably even want to know about your love life."

"I don't really have a love life."

"What about that girl, who you were chasing out of 'The Place' last week?"

Zack finishes the last of his tea before replying, "That's not really my love life. It's more like tearing the scab off an old wound."

"Marie told me that girl is your old girlfriend," Molly replies. "Where did you meet her?"

Zack breathes a deep sigh before saying, "Old girlfriend really isn't an accurate term. I met Abby when I was going to secondary school at the Hanover Conservatory. I played in a string quartet with her. Our second year in the group, it might be fair to say that Abby was my girlfriend. By my last year, Abby was my lover."

"What kind of lover?" Molly asks as she turns herself slightly so that she looks directly into Zack face. Molly continues to hold Zack's right hand.

"The kind that after four months, we stopped being careful and Abby got pregnant."

Zack stops and fiddles with his tea mug, hoping Molly will drop the conservation and ask him if he wants another cup.

"And then?"

"Abby comes from a very well-off family," Zack continues. "We foolishly thought we could save up enough money to run off somewhere and start our life together. After Abby started getting morning sickness, her family discovered that she was pregnant. That same day, her family shipped her to Switzerland for an abortion and then to finishing school. I not only was kicked out of the string quartet but was expelled from Hanover Conservatory and any chance for continuing my education was gone. Coincidently my mom and dad were fired from their jobs with no ability to work anywhere near to Hanover or Halifax."

"So how long ago was this?"

"Almost seven years ago now."

"What happened in those seven years?"

"Last Wednesday was the first time that I have talked with Abby since they shipped her off to Switzerland. On Friday, I met with her. She told me about the abortion, finishing school and getting engaged."

"Is it over with that girl?"

"Maybe."

"How can it be maybe if she's engaged to someone else."

"I'm not really certain what will happen with Abby now," Zack says. "I was not the one who sought out Abby. The only thing of which I am certain is that in the next minute, if Abby texts me, calls me or knocks on your door and says that I need to come with her, I will go with her."

Darkness Arrives

Tuesday, January 21, 12:33AM. Zack wakes up with a start. He remembers dreaming that he was in Fallujah with Clint and Hi. He had just heard Clint shout at him to "put on your battle rattle". He remembers thinking while he was dreaming that it was surprisingly cool for the Al-Hajarah desert. Zack is seated on the couch in the front room of his trailer. He has been sleeping holding on to the guitar as if it were the bullpup which he used to carry in Iraq. After glancing at the wall clock, Zack realizes that he fell asleep sitting up about an hour ago.

Being able to fall asleep sitting up was a skill which Zack acquired in Iraq. He'd been very good at it when he was riding in the swing seat of the APV with Clint and Hi.

Since last Friday, Zack has been returning to Iraq when he drifts off to sleep. The dynamic is causing him to avoid sleeping. Another skill which Zack became very good at in Iraq.

Zack sets his guitar down on the couch, rises and walks to his Nespresso Vertuo on the kitchen counter, making himself a double. He puts two sugar cubes in it and stirs before returning to the couch.

Over the past month, when Zack has not been recording or performing, he has been working on producing songs from his experiences in Iraq. Once he's gotten Abe to create a poem of sorts, rather than having Abe take on producing the lyrics, Zack has taken to doing it himself. The driver for this change has been the amount of time Zack is spending on the songs as well as how fussy he has become about the placement of the words.

Zack drinks half the espresso. He knows that working on these songs is not helping with his current slide into darkness, but he can't help himself. Zack is hoping, as Doc Schiller has told him, getting these songs out of his system may be what he needs to do before he can get on with the rest of his life.

Zack has been thinking a lot about Fallujah the past few days. Twice their APV had been stuck in tricky situations outside of Fallujah. The first when they had a breakdown on a patrol and had to wait 4 hours for support to arrive. After the first hour, as Zack, Clint and Hi sat on the shade-side of their APV, they had been surrounded by a group of young villagers, who seemed intent on getting the trio to fund increasingly expensive food purchases from a nearby kiosk. Having thick black hair and an olive complexion, the locals assumed that Zack was Iraqi and would speak to them in Arabic. This was a common issue Zack had in Iraq when he ran across locals. Some locals would become angry when Zack did not understand what they were saying. A situation which had caused Zack to learn more than a smattering of Arabic during his days in "the Big Suck". In this instance, two of the adolescents believed that Zack was lying to them about not understanding Arabic in order to avoid their demands. Hi, who was the APV's scout and assistant gunner, had finally gotten angry and had driven the kids away. Thirty minutes after the kids left, they began being shot at from behind the stone walls of the Mukhtar Village. Two APV from their squadron had to be sent back to quiet things down. The second incident had been a nasty fire fight with a truck full of jihadis on the desert side of Halabsa. Their APV had just missed being taken out by a rocket from a shoulder launcher.

Zack hears Clint's voice telling him, "It was much worse in the three years before you got here, kid."

"Weren't many days went by that some jihadi wasn't shooting at our asses," Hiram chimes in.

Zack is hearing Clint and Hi's voice more frequently these days. Primarily when he sleeps. Though recently, the voices have come back to him as he works on new songs. Most of what

Zack hears are things which Clint and Hi had said to him at least twenty times. Things such as why Clint and Hi didn't rotate back home, rather than remaining in Iraq for the better part of five years.

"Safer for us in the Big Suck, than it would be back in Brum being chased around by the Johnson Crew," Clint would say.

The story was that Clint and Hi had been drug runners for the Johnson Crew. They brought drugs from the continent to Birmingham. They'd been doing it from the time that they were fifteen. By the time they had turned nineteen, the BrE van which they had been using to transfer auto parts to the continent as a cover, was stopped by an accident in front of them on the Continent side. It was close enough to the Chunnel entrance that a drug-sniffing dog happened by. A pound of raw heroin was discovered in an old transmission casing in the back of the van. After spending four days denying that they knew anything at all about the drugs being there, they finally gave up the name of their two Johnson Crew contacts in return for being allowed to immediately join the Army.

"Wasn't much of a choice," Hiram would say. "Either the slammer for twenty or comin' out here."

"The Big Suck is better than the slammer," Clint would add.

After 5 years, the Johnson Crew still had not forgiven their disloyalty. Every so often one of them would get a typed letter from Birmingham reminding them that the crew was keeping track of their whereabouts.

"Doubtful any of that lot is going to come out here anytime soon and look for us," Hi would say.

Zack had spent the better part of 8 months being with Clint and Hiram 24 hours a day. They ate together. They slept together. They rode in the APV together. The result was that Zack could now hear Clint and Hiram's voices anytime that he wanted, and plenty of times when he didn't want it.

When Zack had been sent back to the Hanover Medical Facility after his injuries in Iraq, he had felt great guilt over having been the only survivor from their APV. Clint and Hiram had been in Iraq for 5 years. Clint and Hiram almost always knew what they were doing. Zack hadn't. What Clint and Hiram knew had saved Zack's ass plenty of times. Yet Clint and Hi were gone, and Zack was still around. Survivor guilt was still around too.

Zack downs the rest of his espresso before he picks up his guitar. He's hoping to record the new song which he has created on Thursday. He has been working on the song for the better part of a week.

Zack begins softly playing where he left off when had fallen asleep earlier.

Fallujah on my mind *12-bar blues at 125 BPM in the Key of C in 4/4 time*

> thick smoke rising in late afternoon
> hope the air jockeys get here soon
> automatic weapon fire breaking the silence
> followed by far off sound of wailing sirens
> hard to get use to the daily grind
> when Fallujah's still stuck in my mind
>
> breathing in choking red dust
> unsure whether in any god I still trust
> everything tastes of burnt cement
> trying to understand where everyone went
> got ourselves into another bind
> another day lost with Fallujah on my mind
>
> not much of anything we won't malign
> after getting ourselves into another bind
> wonder if anything ahead has been mined

retribution comes quick and streamlined
when Fallujah's still stuck in my mind

midday sun keeps beating down
rumbling past a sketchy part of town
gun barrels peak around every corner
piercing eyes make clear we're the foreigner
retribution comes quick and streamlined
when Fallujah's still stuck in my mind

trying to remain alive no matter the cost
no time to track of what's been lost
our conversations filled with profanity
keeps us loose and protects our sanity
isn't much of anything we won't malign
when Fallujah's still stuck in our minds

not much of anything we won't malign
as we get ourselves into another bind
wonder what's up ahead that has been mined
retribution comes quick and streamlined
when Fallujah's still stuck in our minds
with Fallujah stuck in out minds

Unexpected Reunion

Friday, January 24, 10:17PM. Zack and Molly are walking around the back of 'The Shell' after the night's performance.

"Dave says that he emailed you a bill with the charges for the recording sessions that I've done so far out at the studio," Zack says.

"Do you know how much it was?"

"Around $1,700," Zack replies. "He's charging our LLC $100 and hour."

"How many songs does that cover?"

"The three I've recorded so far. I've got another that I'm going to do on Sunday. Likely to be 5 or 6 after that."

"Hey RJ, come on over and say hello," Zack hears from a picnic table just on the other side of the kitchen's outside service counter.

Zack recalls the voice from his past. It is Cindy, the second violin in his old string quartet at Hanover Conservatory. Cindy also used to be Abby's best friend. Zack surveys the table but sees no sign of Abby. Cindy had been one of those with Abby at 'The Place', when Zack had jumped off the stage. Zack walks toward the table where the young blond woman sits. Molly follows along.

"You remember Connie?" Cindy says motioning to the woman on her right.

Connie was the viola player in the quartet. Zack remembers that Connie had not been very friendly to him back in his conservatory days.

Zack nods his head toward Connie.

"This is Brenda," Cindy says. " She teaches primary school with me in Hanover."

Zack turns to Molly and says, "Cindy and Connie were part of the string quartet that I played in during secondary school."

Then turning back to the table, Zack says, "This is Molly Peters, my business partner."

Molly smiles at the girls at the table, links her arm inside of Zack's and says, "I like it better when he just says that I am his partner."

"Why don't you sit down with us for a few minutes and talk about old times?" Cindy says.

Zack curious to see if Cindy has anything to say about Abby, turns to Molly and says, "I'm going to sit with them for a few minutes."

"I've got to go see Marie about this gospel event that we are having on Sunday," Molly says as she moves away from Zack and walks toward 'The Place's' front entrance. "I'll come back out and get you when we're finished."

Zack has agreed to go with Molly to an after-hours place in Wannasea Village where Alfie, who works in the kitchen, is going to be performing.

Zack takes on the empty area at the end of their table. As he does, two women of a similar age come to the table.

"May we have your autograph?" the taller of the two young women asks.

Being asked for autographs has become an increasing feature of Zack's life. It has almost reached the point where he is going to need to stop going into the stores in Wannasea Village. Zack pulls a black, fine point pen out of the inside pocket of his jacket and scrawls his name on the back of the two women's entrance ticket. Signing entrance tickets has become something of a thing for Zack at 'The Place'.

"Sorry," Zack says after he has finished signing the two autographs.

"You've come a long way since our string quartet," Cindy comments.

A young man and woman come to the table and Zack signs their tickets.

"Whatever became of you after the conservatory?" Connie asks. "It was like you were there one minute and gone the next."

Zack finds the question odd. He had tried to talk to any number of people when he was expelled from the conservatory. Cindy and Connie were among them. Neither one would speak to him. It seems extremely unlikely that Cindy doesn't know what happened with Zack at the Conservatory or that she wouldn't have communicated that to Connie.

"I just got tired of playing the cello," Zack says, "and decided it was time to go back to Halifax."

Zack watches as Cindy's eyebrows rise at his statement.

"Where did you go from there?" Connie asks.

"After I finished up secondary," Zack says, "I enlisted in the Army."

"In the middle of the war?" Connie asks.

"Wars are what armies are for," Zack says a little more belligerently than he had actually intended.

"Were you in the war?" Brenda asks.

"Yes," Zack replies, "I spent more than 8 months in Iraq."

Three young women come to the table. Zack gives them autographs.

"How long have you been playing out here?" Brenda asks.

"Going on two years now," Zack replies.

Zack decides he kind of likes Brenda. She doesn't have the upper-class pretention which seems built into Cindy and Connie's being. Not having that pretention was one of those things which Zack had found most alluring about Abby.

"Do you live on the island?" Connie asks.

"I've got a trailer over on the south side," Zack replies.

"Zack was the best cello player that I've ever heard," Connie tells Brenda.

Zack decides that Connie has not heard Abby play cello recently.

"Do you still play?" Cindy asks.

Zack finds the question extremely odd. Evidently Abby has said nothing to Cindy about her trip out to the island to meet him.

"Once in a great while," Zack says. "I'm not quite as good at it now."

"I think you are being modest," Connie says. "RJ had a real future as a cello player."

Two more young women come to the table asking for autographs. Zack complies.

"Is the girl, who was with you, your girlfriend?" Brenda asks.

"She's certainly a friend," Zack says becoming more perverse by the second. "At the moment, she probably is my best friend. Not sure where that leaves us though."

"That's one of the strangest answers that I've ever heard," Brenda says with an impetuous grin.

"It's kind of complicated," Zack replies.

"Have you seen or heard from Abby?" Connie asks.

Zack decides that either Connie is playing games or Cindy has not told her about their meeting at 'The Place'.

"I ran into her a couple weeks ago out here," Zack says. "She seems to be doing well."

"Abby and RJ were a thing," Connie tells Brenda.

It's Zack's turn to raise his eyebrows and hope that Molly will soon be on her way back.

"Abby's getting married," Cindy says, "you know."

"I do know," Zack says a little too quickly.

A couple comes to the table. Zack completes their autograph request.

"You certainly are popular," Brenda says. "Does signing autographs annoy you?"

"It's just part of the business," Zack says. "I see it as a way to say 'thank you' to my fans. Without those fans, I would still be bartending."

Zack sees Molly coming out of the side kitchen entrance. Rarely has Zack been so glad to see Molly. Although recently, Zack is becoming increasingly happy that Molly is around. Molly seems to help ward off the darkness.

"I've got to run," Zack says rising from the table. "We are going down to the village to see one of the kids, who works out here, perform. It's been very good to see and meet everyone."

"Good to see you, too," Cindy says. "Why don't you come out to the next conservatory reunion when we have it this summer."

"I'll try to," Zack lies, knowing the chances that he will receive an invitation for that reunion are non-existent.

"Would you mind autographing our tickets before you go?" Brenda asks.

Zack signs their entrance tickets, then hustles to Molly and guides her out to the back of the parking lot where his battered VW is parked.

"How did your little reunion go?" Molly as they walk across the parking lot.

"Strange," Zack replies. "Actually, stranger than strange."

"What was strange about it?"

"Either the one named Cindy was doing surveillance," Zack replies, "or those three were just after autographs."

Zack presses the button on the VW's fob to unlock it.

"Where's this place Alfie is playing?" Zack asks.

"It's called 'Herb's" Molly replies. "It's about two blocks down Main from 'Archie's'."

Zack starts up the Bug and wheels it out of the parking lot. He turns left down familiar Mountain Way toward the village.

"You don't sound like you like those girls very much," Molly said.

"The two girls, who I was in the Hanover Conservatory with, had no use for me when I was there," Zack says. "They were always telling Abby to stay away from me, dump me or worse. Now suddenly, they are my fans."

"See your music is magic," Molly says with a laugh. "Like time, your music seems able to heal wounds."

"You don't really believe that do you?"

Molly thinks for a long moment before answering, "No."

Zack swings the VW around the Main Street traffic circle to the left exit.

"Think we should park in the city garage?" Zack asks.

"Probably a good idea," Molly says. "I don't think there is much parking down by Herb's."

Zack goes two blocks and swings left into the parking garage. The lower floor is practically empty.

As they walk through the garage, Molly takes Zack's hand. In silence they walk the two blocks west to a small clapboard building which used to sell women's clothes. There are quite a few young people of various genders milling about in front of the bar. Zack notices that more than a few of them are pointing at him and whispering. Molly hurries him through the entrance to where the bouncer/doorman is selling tickets.

"Say you're Zack Tillerman, aren't you?" the doorman comments as he takes a $20 bill from Molly then stamps both of their hands.

"Guilty," Zack says with a sheepish smile.

"There's a table in the back reserved for you," the doorman says. "Ask Ginger at the bar to show you the way."

Molly and Zack go the bar, where a late twenties something woman with fiery red hair in a tight fitting deep scarlet evening dress is serving drinks.

"Be with you in a minute," the redhead says.

The bar is crowded. Molly leans into Zack. If Zack is being honest with himself, he no longer minds Molly leaning into him.

Complete with filling drink orders, the redhead comes back and says, "You're Zack, I'm guessing. I'm Ginger. Follow me."

Ginger guides them to a table at the far end of the bar.

A transgender male dressed to the nines is on the small stage singing Peggy Lee's "Fever". A MultiTracks Player provides the accompaniment.

"What can I get you?" Ginger asks.

"Rum and coke," Molly replies.

"Jameson and water for me," Zack says.

Ginger disappears to the bar.

"They do two Drag nights a week here," Molly says. "One on Tuesday. One on Friday."

"How many times has Alfie performed here?" Zack asks.

"This will be his second time," Molly replies.

Ginger returns with their drinks.

"Herb says the drinks are on him," Ginger says.

"Tell Herb that I said thanks very much," Zack says.

"You just did," Ginger says as she smiles alluringly at Zack then walks back to the bar.

Molly and Zack sip their drinks through the sets of next two singers. Zack gets the impression that the songs are more about impersonating the look and actions of the singers than the actual music production.

"Here's Alfie," Molly whispers.

Zack is vaguely able to determine that the lanky, barefoot, bronze-complected young woman in the flower dress is the same Alfie, who he has seen working in the kitchen at 'The Place'.

"Who is Alfie supposed to be?" Zack whispers in Molly's ear.

"Lana Del Rey," Molly replies. "Do you know her?"

"Not really," Zack replies.

"Look her up when you have a chance," Molly says.

Alfie breaks into "Blue Jeans". Zack doesn't know about Alfie's appearance, but the song sounds eerily familiar to a song he's been hearing on the VW's radio.

Alfie follows up with "Dark Paradise". Zack is less familiar with this song, but he likes what he is hearing.

Alfie exits the stage to a ringing round of applause.

"Let's stay until she does her finale for the night," Molly says.

They sat through the first 3 more performers, two of whom had been on the stage before. Alfie returns in a wide pinstriped suit and tie with a short blond wig holding a cigarette in his right hand.

"Do you know who Alfie is channeling?" Molly whispers into Zack's ear.

"No clue," Zack whispers back.

"Marlene Dietrich," Molly says.

Zack recalls the name. He thinks it has something to do with one of the two world wars. He remembers his grandmother watching black and white films which he thinks might have had someone named Marlene Dietrich in them.

Alfie sings "Lilli Marlene" complete with German-accented English before doing the song in German. To the crowd's delight, Alfie vamps his rather remarkable legs and gestures with the cigarette as she sings.

The crowd cheers and claps when the song is finished.

Alfie rounds out his evening with "Falling in Love Again" bringing the house down when Alfie does the line, "I was made that way". The crowd roars as Alfie exits the stage.

"Damn," Zack says, "Alfie is good."

"You ought to hear her do you in the kitchen," Molly says with a laugh.

Solo

Sunday, January 26, 12:02PM. Zack is in the SouthTown recording studio going over a new song which he had just finished late last night. This is the first song which Zack is going to have recorded which he has written by himself.

Dave and Abe walk through the side entrance door. Zack exits the recording area and goes into the control room as the NorthEnders continue to work on the song as they have been for the past two hours.

Zack is visibly nervous as he shakes hands first with Abe and then Dave.

"We are ready to take a first cut," Zack says to Dave. Then turning to Abe, adds, "If there is anything you don't like or think ought to be changed with the lyrics, tell Dave to stop the recording and signal me."

"Will do," Abe says.

Zack returns to the recording area, closes the door and says to the band, "Let's give it a go."

Dark Thoughts Come *108 BPM in key of G Minor in 4/4 time*

memories too real to reject
take over every aspect
of each living hour
for this being they devour
this guitar strums
as dark thoughts come

my will to carry on
is suddenly gone
dread becomes limitless
explosions the stimulus

sounds from far-off guns
as dark thoughts come

whose time is it to die
under the blue Anbar sky
as our ride is blown to bits
just the other side of Hit
there will be a settling of sums
when dark thoughts come

how much more self-abuse
will memory shake loose
cannot find peace
any sense of release
with unresolved outcomes
as the dark thoughts come

completely helpless
caught up in wartime mess
where everything collides
leaving shattered lives
will to carry on succumbs
as dark thoughts come

before we'll find peace
or some sense of release
the will to carry on
very suddenly gone
this guitar strums
as dark thoughts come

feel completely helpless
lost in this wartime mess
cannot find peace
or any sense of release
this guitar strums
as dark thoughts come

> how much more self-abuse
> will memory shake loose
> this guitar strums
> as dark thoughts come
>
> shall be no peace
> no sense of relief
> this guitar strums
> as dark thoughts come

After the first run through Zack looks out at Abe and puts his hands up in front of his face in a questioning gesture.

Abe gives him a thumbs up with his right hand.

"Let's do it again to see what we've got," Dave says through the microphone at the control station.

Zack and the band do the song three more times before Dave is satisfied. Zack comes back into the control room immediately after Dave has finished the fourth recording.

"That's disquieting stuff," Dave exclaims to Zack as he enters the control room.

"Abe?" Zack says with Abe's opinion being the one which he really wants to hear.

Abe turns around and faces Zack, looking him directly in the eyes.

"I've spent the past twenty-five years trying to describe what it feels like when that darkness you just sang about comes," Abe says. "You just did it on your first attempt."

"Really?"

"Really," Abe confirms.

Jerome, the NorthEnders' lead pokes his head out of the recording studio and says, "Are we good?"

"You're better than good," Dave says as he brings the 3rd recording of the song up on the studio's audio system.

"You really need to get the song up on your website," Dave says.

"We decided that we are going to wait until we have the rest of the Iraq songs done," Zack says.

"That song is too good to sit on," Dave says.

"I'm with Dave," Abe adds.

"I don't want to put it up there without running it past Molly first," Zack insists.

"I think she's tied up with that gospel thing they are doing at 'The Shell' this morning," Abe says.

Zack pulls his cell phone out of his pocket.

"Maybe she's finished by now," Zack says as he dials her number.

The phone rings four times before Molly answers.

"We're just finishing up with this gospel event," Molly says. "Can I call you back?"

"Will you give me three minutes now?" Zack asks.

"It will cost you," Molly says with a laugh.

"I'll pay," Zack says before he explains what Dave and Abe have said about the new song.

"Can you play it for me?" Molly asks when Zack is finished with the explanation.

"Can you put the song on again?" Zack asks Dave as he switches the phone to speaker.

Dave complies as Molly listens to the song through her cell phone.

"Wow," Molly says into the cellphone when the song is finished. "I'm not sure that I'm getting all of it, but I think Abe and Dave are right."

"I'll have Dave get with you to set it up on the website," Zack says. "Do you think I should add any kind of introduction to the song so people will know there are other Iraqi blues songs coming?"

"I wouldn't worry about that right now," Molly says. "Ask Dave to send me a copy of it. I'd like Beth and Marie to hear it."

"Okay," Zack says. "Are you coming out to the trailer later?"

"In a couple hours," Molly replies. "Who wrote that thing?"

Zack hesitates a few moments before saying, "I did."

"By yourself?"

"By myself."

Restructuring

Wednesday, January 29, 10:52AM. Molly and Zack walk into the glass door entrance of the Meeting Center at Mountain Village. They walk to the front counter where Annette is huddled with the young lady who works at the desk on the weekends. There are six people seated in sofa chairs in the lobby area.

"Hey guys," Annette says looking up from the computer screen which she is reviewing. "Be with you in a minute. Why don't you grab a coffee from the serving bar."

Zack and Molly walk to where Annette has pointed.

"Pretty fancy," Zack says to Molly as they walk to the serving area. "Have you been in here before?"

"I'm spending most of my working life during the week in here now," Molly replies. "Beats the heck out of the storage room office over at 'The Place'."

Zack pours himself a cup of coffee and puts two sugars in it. Molly is in the process of steeping a cup of herbal tea when Annette walks up to them.

"Let's go to the little meeting room upstairs," Annette advises.

Zack and Molly follow her up the stairs.

"Kind of busy today," Molly remarks.

"We have a couple seminars being done by Swansea University going on through Saturday," Annette says. "This is the first time that we've had most of the tiny houses and rooms booked."

They enter a 12'X18' meeting room which seats six.

"Make yourselves comfortable," Annette instructs as she exits the room. "Abe said he might be a few minutes late. He has to wait for Olivia."

"Do you know why Olivia might be coming?" Zack asks Molly.

"Not a clue."

The pair seat themselves on the two rolling chairs at the end of the dark walnut conference table. Zack and Molly believe the purpose of this meeting is to discuss what to do about the ZackTillerman.com website which has not been able to handle the volume of sales traffic which has resulted from 'Dark Thoughts Come'. The website has crashed three times since Monday afternoon.

"I've lost track of the number of requests that are on the website either for interviews or asking you to appear on various radio and tv shows," Molly tells Zack after taking a sip of her tea. "You really need to consider doing a few of them." Zack grimaces. At the moment, he is still only able to put his mind on working on new Iraqi Blues music. The only other thing Zack seems capable of focusing upon is performing. Sleep for Zack has become a fleeting thing which usually results in waking up in a cold sweat.

"I'd be willing to do a couple interviews over the phone," Zack says.

"That's not going to fly," Molly says. "How about if I see if I can arrange for a few of them to come out here and interview you?"

Zack sips his coffee and remains noncommittal.

"What did you say the last sales total for 'Dark Thoughts Come' was?" Zack asks, hoping to move Molly away from the topic of interviews.

"When I checked at 9," Molly replies, "It was a little over 170,000."

"How much do we make from that?"

"I had Dave set the price for that song at $1.29," Molly says. "We end up with about $.98 profit from each sale."

"That's a lot of money," Zack says shaking his head and sipping his coffee.

"It's also breaking our website," Molly replies.

"What does the internet company say about it?" Zack asks.

"Dave says the only viable options at the moment are either to increase our website bandwidth or move the song to some other sales channels like Amazon Music," Molly replies.

"What will that cost?" Zack asks.

"We would have to commit to paying about $2,400 per month for our internet service for the next year," Molly replies. "Moving to other sales channel will likely reduce our take on the sales by at least 25%."

"Damned if we do," Zack says in almost the same way Clint used to say it, "Damned if we don't."

"Something like that," Molly says. "What's clear is we cannot continue to conduct our business as we have been."

"I'm not all that sure that I want to conduct business," Zack replies. "I'm just interested in making and playing music."

Molly sighs.

"Do you have any idea what Abe is thinking we should do?" Zack asks.

Molly shakes her head and pulls her cell phone out of the jacket pocket. She begins going through text messages.

"Dave says the website crashed again this morning," Molly says. "We have to decide what we are going to do about it."

Zack takes another sip of his coffee before saying, "How do we know that the sales from 'Dark Thoughts Come' won't drop off soon and our current website will work just fine?"

"We don't," Molly says. "We also don't know that the sales won't increase, and our website will become completely useless."

"Why don't we run just 'Dark Thoughts Come' through one of the music services?" Zack asks.

"There's a thought," Molly says. "See, you can do business if you try."

Zack can do many things, but the only thing which he really wants to do right now is write 'Iraqi Blues' music.

Olivia and Abe come into the conference room.

After hellos are exchanged, Abe and Olivia sit down next to Molly and Zack.

"Seems like you guys have a good problem," Abe says.

"It may be good," Molly replies with a frown, "but it is still a problem which has to be addressed immediately."

"Before we get into that problem," Abe says, "I think it best if we deal with something else first. It's why I have brought Olivia along."

"Okay," Molly says hesitantly.

Zack sips coffee.

"In March," Abe says, "I'm planning on dropping out of ZackTillerman LLC."

Zack stops sipping coffee and focuses on Abe. Molly's jaw drops slightly.

"I'm too old for this business," Abe continues. "I've become focused on historical writing, Alice's journals, and my presentations. I am now fully confident Zack can create his own songs three times better than I am able if he sets his mind to it. I'm also certain that you guys are at the point where you are either going to need to get serious about this ZackTillerman thing or end up sliding backwards."

Zack and Molly are silent.

"In December," Abe goes on, "I had Olivia help me redo my will. With the Twins coming along and the money I came into from the lawsuit, I really had no other choice. As part of my new will, I decided that I am going to leave ZackTillerman LLC all the rights to the lyrics which I have produced over the years. The first part of this year, when I finally decided that I am going to drop out of ZackTillerman, I figured that it really doesn't make sense to wait until I am gone to turn those rights over. I'm going to do it as soon as Olivia can help us figure out the best way to go about it."

"You aren't going to work with us anymore?" Zack says in disbelief.

"You can ask my opinion on anything, anytime that you want," Abe says, "but as far as the day-to-day operation of ZackTillermanLLC, I would like to be out no later than the middle of March."

Unmoored

Thursday, January 30, 10:12AM. Molly and Zack are sitting in the control room area of the SouthTown studio waiting for Dave. Yesterday after taking a few hours to digest Abe dropping out of ZackTillermanLLC, they had decided to move 'Dark Thoughts Come' along with whatever ends up being what Zack is calling the 'Iraqi Blues' album to a music distribution service. Molly and Zack then agreed that they will restructure their LLC with the thought of including Dave in the company if he is interested. They have also hired Olivia as their legal advisor. Olivia has advised them to work out what they want to do with the ownership stakes in the LLC, then she will review and help them make it happen it if is feasible. Last evening after the performance at 'The Place', they had decided to sleep on their thinking and get together at the studio this morning.

Zack is also at the studio to do his next recording for 'Iraqi Blues'. Zack is anxious to put the restructuring of the LLC behind him as quickly as possible.

"I'd like to bring Dave in to help me with reviewing the new songs which I create," Zack says.

"Does Dave know anything about lyric development?" Molly asks.

"Probably just as much as I do,' Zack replies. "Dave does have a good ear."

"Is he going to have the time to give you to help with that as well as run this studio?" Molly asks.

"I think if we give him 10% of ZackTillerman," Zack says, "he should have enough income to hire somebody to help with the non-recording end of this studio."

"That's a big assumption on your part,' Molly says with a frown. "Have you talked to Dave about this at all?"

"No," Zack replies, "but I was thinking that we could offer him 10% of the LLC from what Abe is giving back to us."

"Are you thinking 15% of the LLC for me, 10% for Dave and the rest belongs to you?"

"Actually, I was thinking 20% for you," Zack replies.

Molly shakes her head.

"You have to stop giving things away," Molly says. "15% for handling the finances and business management task is more than fair. With the income which we are currently getting from 'Dark Thoughts Come', I think 10% is too much for basically being your song writing sounding board. I would suggest 5% maximum."

"How about 7.5%," Zack asks.

Molly does some calculations on her cellphone before saying, "I'd be okay with 7 percent."

"Let's offer him that then," Zack replies.

Are you planning on charging Dave anything for getting that percentage of our LLC?"

"I don't think Dave can afford to invest anything else after what he has put into this place," Zack says.

"We are going to need to pay Abe back for the $10,000 which he put into the LLC to start it up," Molly says. "If we are going to do this, why don't we ask Dave to work off that $10K from his first few profit distributions?"

"You can run it past him," Zack says.

"When will we want these changes to go into effect?"

"I'm thinking March," Zack says. "Right now, I'm hoping to have 'Blues' complete by the end of February. I'd like to have Dave's help in doing that."

"I think that will be too hard to set up," Molly says. "Why don't we make April 1 the goal and see if Olivia thinks that is feasible."

"Let's see what Dave thinks," Zack says as he begins leafing through some hand-written sheets of music which he has been working on.

For the next 20 minutes, Molly responds to text and website messages while Zack's works on the song.

"Sorry," Dave says coming through the door which leads to the retail sales area of the studio. "I had to wait until Sam got here to run the front counter. What is it that you want to meet with me about?"

Molly explains Abe's plans to leave their LLC early next month.

"We'd like to see if you want to consider coming in with us?" Zack says.

Dave looks at him quizzically, "How would that work?"

"You would basically assume Abe's role in helping me develop and review songs," Zack says, "and receive a percentage of our LLC in return."

"How much time does Abe usually put in on that?" Dave asks.

"Sometimes ten hours a week," Zack says. "Sometimes as much as twenty hours a week. I kind of work around Abe's schedule. I could do the same for you."

"About the only time that I would have for anything like that would be after the store closes at 7," Dave says. " Assuming that someone hasn't' contracted us to handle their audio work at a performance."

"With the income you'd get from the LLC, maybe you could hire someone to run the store?" Zack says. "Then we could work on songs during the day?"

"How much income are we talking about?" Dave asks.

"We are proposing that you get 7% of the LLC. Before 'Dark Thoughts Come', the profit from that percentage of ownership has been running about $2-3,000 per month," Molly replies. "With our new sales numbers, I'd expect that to be quite a bit more."

"When would this ownership start?" Dave asks.

"We are thinking the first of April," Molly says. "We need to work out the legal aspect of the deal with Olivia. I can let you have a copy of the past year of our financials if you'd like?"

Dave thinks for a few moments, "Seeing the financials would be great. Why don't you have Olivia work out what I would need to commit to signing? If I'm still interested after going through your offer, can we talk about it then?"

"Sounds good to me," Zack says.

"I'll get with Olivia to work out a draft agreement," Molly says.

Dave begins preparing his equipment for recording.

"Did you guys have any idea Abe was thinking of retiring from the music business?" Dave asks while he adjusts the board.

"I had a suspicion," Molly says. "There were too many things Abe kept saying about how he needed to spend more time at the Historical Society working on the journals and the sessions at the Historical Society which he is going to start giving shortly."

"I didn't suspect anything," Zack says.

"You said you want to do a recording?" Dave asks.

"Yes," Zack replies. "I've got another standalone song which I want to record. Do you have time to record it now?"

"I do," Dave says. "Why don't you go in the studio, get ready, and I'll get things set up here.

Zack rises from his chair in the back of the control room and goes into the recording studio closing the door behind him.

"Zack isn't into dealing very well with Abe leaving," Dave says to Molly, "is he?"

"Nope," Molly says. "As far as Zack is concerned, any time spent away from writing or producing songs is a waste of time."

"I don't think Zack has a clue how much time he actually spends producing new songs," Dave says off-handedly. 'The past few weeks, he and Abe have been in here working on songs more often than not and I'm not just talking about during business hours."

"Zack is really going to miss Abe," Molly says as Dave prepares to do the recording.

"I'm ready when you are," Dave says into the control room microphone.

Zack, who is seated on a stool in front of a dynamic microphone, nods his head and positions his fingers on his acoustic guitar.

what we do to ourselves *159 BPM in the key of G Major in 6/8 time*

> patriotism, a cause to be upheld
> serving their nation, they all felt compelled

battle's where they learn for themselves
war is what we do to ourselves

they were not advised
they would be despised
in a land which doesn't want them there
if none survive, who's really going to care?

signing on to be overwhelmed
war is what we do to ourselves
battle's where they learn for themselves
war is what we do to ourselves

they swore an oath
which killed them both
they were not told
they wouldn't grow old
war's not what's read upon bookshelves
war is what we do to ourselves

no matter how far in history anyone delves
war's always been what we do to ourselves
war will always be what we do to ourselves

crumpled up and thrown away
small price for nations to pay
to claim moral superiority
human lives, a lower priority
battle's where they learn for themselves
war is what we do to ourselves

hand-held missiles streaking round
500lb bombs raining down
target a housing complex
eliminate any who object
chemical weapons with nobody's blessing
implements of an ethnic cleansing

citing lessons military protocol compels
war becomes what we do to ourselves
in battle all soon learn for themselves
war is what we do to ourselves

big guns attached to metal turret
IEDs planted throughout the desert
military equipment is not made by elves
war becomes what we do to ourselves

no matter how far into history anyone delves
war will always be what we do to ourselves
war's always what we do to ourselves

Big Time

Monday, February 3, 2:18PM. The sun is bright. The breeze which blows up from the ocean is cool and crisp. Molly and Zack are seated at the picnic table closest to the parking lot at 'The Place'. They are waiting for the arrival of Roger Watters, principal owner of the Mainland Talent Agency, the largest such firm on the Mainland. Waters has been using various methods to contact Molly over the past month to describe how his company would be able to expand and enhance Zack Tillerman's musical career. Abe had suggested to Molly that it probably wouldn't be a bad idea to meet with Watters to understand what options he can offer for the future of ZackTillerman LLC. After two somewhat heated phone conversations, Molly was able to talk Zack into meeting with him. Waters has agreed to come out to the place at 2:30 this afternoon.

"Who is this guy again?" Zack asks as he takes a sip from the cup of coffee which Molly has brought him from the Meeting Center.

"Abe says that he runs the largest talent agency on the Mainland," Molly says. "If nothing else, he should be able to give us an idea of how we might be able to grow ZackTillerman LLC."

"Why is it that we want to grow?" Zack says. "I'm actually more worried about getting too big and losing focus on the music."

"I think Roger Watters will be able to explain how his organization would help us grow as well as being able to make certain that doesn't happen," Molly says.

"What did you tell me that our last sales for 'Dark Thoughts Come' is up to?" Zack asks.

"Almost 285,000," Molly replies.

"That isn't enough growth for you?" Zack counters.

"That is an opportunity," Molly says, "which you ought to be taking more advantage of."

"How much money are we going to net out of those sales?" Zack asks.

"Probably around $200,000," Molly says.

"How long have we had the song for sale?" Zack asks.

"A little over a week," Molly says.

"Throw in every one of my booking dates at 'The Place' which are open for sales have been sold out as they are offered. How much more do you want?"

"Top selling artists sell millions of recordings in a week," Molly replies.

"I'm not a top selling artist," Zack says. "I'm a hard-working musician on a little island, who has been lucky enough to sell a few records. Honestly, I'm not really interested in much more than that."

"Broaden your horizons," Molly says.

Zack stands up from the picnic table. He stretches his arms out wide and begins pointing as he says, "I've got the mountain up there. I've got the lakes over there. The village is down there. There are twenty-two beaches on the island. We are surrounded by the sea. I like my horizons just fine where they are."

Molly frowns before countering, "Then maybe you need to get off this island more often and look around a little. There is a whole planet out there. A planet, which if you do things right, would probably like to hear your music. That is if they actually had a chance to know about it."

"If they want music like mine," Zack says, "all they have to do is look on the internet for it."

Zack picks up his empty paper coffee cup and carries it to the trash receptacle.

"You have the potential to be something more," Molly says.

"I'm not looking to be anything more," Zack says. "I like living in my trailer. I like going to the beach every morning. I like doing three performances a week. I like writing new songs when I feel like it. That's more than enough for me."

"Someday maybe you are going to have kids," Molly says. "I'll bet those kids will want something more than what you just described. I know for certain that they aren't going want to be riding around in that beat up thing you call a car."

"If there are ever kids," Zack replies shaking his head, "I'll cross that bridge when I get to it. Until then I'll continue to drive the Bug and be satisfied with being able to call my own shots in the music business."

Molly's cell phone rings. It's the music agent. He has just docked at the ferry. Molly explains where they are sitting and that they are the only people on the patio.

"Roger will be here in a few minutes," Molly says. "Please promise me that you will listen to what he has to say."

"I promise that I will listen," Zack replies, "but I will not promise that it is going to do anything to change my mind."

Zack sits down at the picnic table before saying, "During my session with Doc Schiller this morning, I had a thought about what we might do with the rollout of the 'Iraqi Blues' album when it's finished."

Molly wrinkles her eyebrows at Zack.

"I suggested to Doc that when I finish up the album, the first thing that I'd like to do is play the album at a benefit concert at their medical facility. I'll do some songs other than Iraqi Blues of course."

This is the first thing Zack has said today which pleases Molly.

"That's sounds like a great idea," Molly replies.

"Doc said he could put us in touch with the right people to talk to about it," Zack says.

"You are actually willing to do a performance off the island?

"At the Hanover Medical Facility sure," Zack replies. "Anywhere else, no."

"Please ask Doc Schiller to give you the information on who we should contact to make arrangements for the concert," Molly requests. "I will set things up from there, once you know for sure when the album is going to be ready."

A green Jaguar XF pulls into the parking lot and pulls up beside Zack's battered VW,

A slim, tall man, who looks to be in his early forties dressed in blue jeans, black silk shirt, an AMG team cap carrying a leather briefcase, exits the car and walks to their table.

"I'm glad you agreed to meet with me," the agent says. "Particularly on a beautiful day like this."

After exchanging introductions, the agent hands Molly and Zack a glossy brochure which outlines the services his company provides to musicians.

"I've been in the music talent business for seventeen years," Watters tells Zack as they sit down at the picnic table. "I've never run across a talent quite as unique as you."

"Thanks," Zack says sheepishly.

"Molly tells me that you have become somewhat overwhelmed by your sudden success," Watters says. "I believe that is something my team can certainly help with."

"Actually," Zack interjects, "right now, I think the loss of my songwriting partner has hurt us more than anything else."

Watters gives Zack an odd look, "Somebody died?"

"No," Molly says, "Abe Stolz has been working with Zack as his talent manager and lyricist. He's just turned 72 and has decided that he wants to devote the rest of his life to teaching and writing island history."

"Abe Stolz," the agents says as he ponders the name, "isn't he the guy that wrote those Tara Rose songs about thirty years ago?"

"Along with most of the music Reggie Reginald did," Molly adds.

"Reggie Reginald," the agent muses. "The Wannasea legend. Seems he got himself in a spot of trouble a little while back."

"He is now serving a 40-year term for drug smuggling and associated crimes in the Swansea Prison," Molly states.

"Did Stolz write the lyrics for 'Dark Thoughts Come'?" Watters asks.

"No," Zack says somewhat hesitantly, "I wrote those lyrics, but Abe helped me fine tune them."

"Are you really looking for more of an artistic guide in the songwriting area then?" the agent postures.

"I'm not sure we know what we are looking for," Molly says.

Zack decides he's better off being silent.

"My agency can certainly help you out in any aspect of songwriting that you may need," Watters adds. "From reviewing your work before production up to having one of today's best songwriters produce songs suited to your talent."

Watters launches into a fifteen-minute animated description of the services which the Mainland Talent Agency offers.

"We will provide you with every available tool to prepare you for success," Watters says. "The rest will be up to you and your music."

"What are your fees?" Molly asks.

"20% off the top once you reach rate," Watters replies.

"What is rate?" Zack asks.

"It's at least $250,000 per year in sales," Watters says. "We give an artist a set period of time to reach rate. Until they do, we only take 10%. From what Molly tells me, you are already exceeding rate."

"What happens if an artist doesn't reach rate?" Zack asks.

"Normally for a period of about 6 months," Watters says, "we develop a strict regimen to try to get the artist to hit rate. If that doesn't work out, normally we will amicably part ways."

"What about bookings?" Molly asks.

"If you sign with us," Watters says, "we will manage all of your bookings."

"How much say would have in those bookings?" Zack asks.

"As much as is reasonable except when it would impede your career," Watters answers.

"Currently," Molly says, "Zack is booked to play 3 days per week here."

"That's probably something which we could live with for a few months," Watters replies. "We'd immediately want to start booking you into bigger venues. Particularly when you have new recordings coming out."

"I really have no interest in doing performances in any other venue," Zack injects.

"Molly mentioned this," Watters says. "I'm hoping that I can make you understand why that is not going to help you advance your career. Music tends to be a brutal business. One month you have a hit song or album. Two months later sales drop off. In six months, nobody remembers you or your songs. I can help you to avoid that."

"Mr. Watters," Zack says, "you certainly appear to be very competent and knowledgeable about the music business. I'm certain that for someone in the music business driven by financial success, your agency is a boon. Being completely honest with you however, beyond people enjoying what I sing and being able to create a few songs once in a while, I really have all the success that I want at the moment."

"I will tell you from experience," Watters says, "that musicians, who think that way, usually end up as buskers or worse. If they are lucky, they play on a corner where there are large crowds. I don't think this island is known for its large crowds."

"If I end up a year from now playing my guitar down by the ferry docks for what people leave in my guitar case," Zacks says, "I will be fine with that."

"Zack," Watters answers, "I am not exaggerating when I say this, you are literally throwing millions of dollars away."

"Millions of dollars," Zack responds, "is not going to get me where I am hoping to go. Playing my music, my way, will."

Back to Iraq

Thursday, February 6, 10:04AM. Zack is seated in the control room of the SouthTown studio with Dave. The NorthEnders are in the studio warming up in preparation for Zack recording two new Iraqi Blues songs which he had finished up yesterday.

"Molly says that you are thinking of doing a concert over at the Hanover Medical Facility," Dave says to Zack as he turns on the control panel.

"As soon as I get this album finished," Zack says, "I'm hoping to do a free concert over there."

"I'd like to be involved as much as you'll let me," Dave says.

"That will be great," Zack says. "I'm not sure what kind of equipment we are going to need to haul over there. Molly is working on finding out. I'll ask her to get with you once we have the specifics."

"When do you think this concert is going to be?" Dave asks.

"If I stay on track to finish this album," Zack replies, "probably the second or third week of March."

"How many songs are you planning for Iraqi Blues?" Dave asks.

"I'm thinking ten right now," Zack says, "but that is going to depend on how I feel when I get to the tenth one."

Zack rises from the control room bench and says, "I think the guys are ready."

Zack goes into the recording studio and picks up his electric guitar. After two or three minutes of working out the tuning, Zack nods his head to Dave, who begins recording.

quicksand of time *91 BPM in key of A Major in 4/4 time*

environment where nothing is fair
soot and residue blow everywhere
living lives full of grit and grime
lost in depths of the quicksand of time

desert full of swirling dust
skin soon grows a second crust
thought of hot shower becomes sublime
got ourselves lost in the quicksand of time

sands of time
shifting sands of time
got ourselves lost
in the quicksand of time

when the order comes it's up we'll climb
wouldn't have thought we'd end up here
hiding in shadows filled with fear
lost in muck of the quicksand of time

trying to overcome stress
of being the matter of who loses less
deciding what constitutes a war crime
becoming lost in the quicksand of time

sands of time
shifting sands of time
got ourselves lost
in the quicksand of time

swirling winds and moving dunes
we won't be home anytime soon
there's no pay for overtime
when lost in the quicksand of time

sands of time
shifting sands of time
got ourselves lost
in the quicksand of time

> living a life full of grit and grime
> when the order comes, it's up I'll climb
> there'll be no pay for overtime
> when we're lost in the quicksand of time
>
> living a life full of grit and grime
> when the order comes, it's up I'll climb
> there'll be no pay for overtime
> when we've lost ourselves in the quicksand of time
> when we've lost ourselves in this quicksand of time

The group does the song four times before Zack is satisfied with the result.

Zack turns to the NorthEnders and asks, "Do you guys have time to do the other one?"

Jerome nods his head affirmatively before handing out the sheet music Zack has created for the next song.

"Why don't you guys get ready for it," Zack says as he walks back into the control room. "Let me know if there is anything which you think ought to be changed."

"Well?" Zack asks Dave.

"I know this is kind of weird thing to say for this type of music," Dave says, "but that song is kind of catchy."

"Wasn't my intention to be catchy," Zack says furrowing his brow.

"I wouldn't worry about it," Dave says. "The song makes its point. I think however that line "there will be no pay for overtime" is going to end up stuck in a lot of people's minds."

"I spent a good deal of time with Abe on that song," Zack says. "I ended up changing it around at least fifty different times."

"It's a great song," Dave says. "Let's put it away and do the other one."

"Probably a good idea," Zack says. "I tend to get too fixated on a song when I'm creating it. Abe tells me I need to learn how to let go. He says that it is like raising children. You try to do the best you can while you are developing the song but there comes a time where you just have to let go of it to see they are capable of standing on their own."

Jerome comes out to the control room and goes over two proposed changes from the group. Zack agrees to both.

"I want to make sure this next one has a lot of bass in it," Zack tells Dave. "I'd like it to sound somewhat similar to that fuzzy sound on the Stones' "Paint it Black"."

"Let's give it a shot," Dave says.

Zack returns to the recording studio. He and the group go over the first six bars, three times before they agree on the sound.

Zack nods to Dave. Dave begins recording.

Gunbarrel Blues *159BPM in the key of B in 3/4 time*

taught me to shoot straight and fast
to not talk back and do what's asked
bullpup strapped upon my back
along with this jacket they say stops flak
what's a poor boy supposed to do
when he's caught a case of gunbarrel blues

learned real quick not to think
how to make my very soul shrink
so when we point our weapon
at a target there will be no guessin'
what's a poor boy supposed to do
when he's caught a case of gunbarrel blues

when into trouble I'll soon be steppin'
there's little comfort in the stock of my weapon
blue steel muzzle glows white and hot
when something's out there which must be shot
what's a poor boy supposed to do
when he's come down with a bad case of gunbarrel blues

no thought to be given
no matter how far we have driven
from the safety of our camp
huddled in the darkness, light no lamp
what's a poor boy supposed to do
when he's come down with a case of gunbarrel blues

taught me to shoot straight and fast
to not talk back and do what's asked
bullpup strapped upon my back
along with this jacket they say stops flak
what's a poor boy supposed to do
when he's got a bad case of gunbarrel blues

what's a poor boy supposed to do
when he's caught a bad case of gunbarrel blues

what's a poor boy supposed to do
when he's stuck with a case of gunbarrel blues

what's a poor boy supposed to do
when he comes down with a case of gunbarrel blues

A Different Course

Sunday, February 9, 12:54PM. Zack is parking his battered VW in the lot of 'The Place'. Molly has asked him to talk with Alfie, who has just turned 17 and has decided that he is going drop out of school and take up an offer a club called 'Jewel's' in Halifax to perform 5 nights a week. At the moment Alfie is in the kitchen helping Sallie finish up lunch service for a Swansea University Convention which will be held on 'The Four Pillars of Sustainability' in 'the Shell'.

Noticing that quite a few people are milling about the patio area, Zack walks around the other side of the building and enters 'The Place' through the rear door. He walks into the kitchen, where Sallie, Randy and Alfie are working on cleaning up the pots and pans as Judith and Jennifer tend the counter at the patio window.

"Hey guys," Zack calls out as he comes through the kitchen door and walks toward Sallie. He nods and waves to each of the staff as they respond to him.

"Is it okay if I take Alfie away from you for a while," Zack says as he walks up behind Sallie.

"Sure," Sally says. "I'm hoping you can talk some sense into her. Seventeen is too young to be going off to the Mainland by yourself. Particularly without any type of educational certification."

Molly had told Zack that Beth and Marie had both tried to dissuade Alfie from taking up the Jewel's offer, but neither been able to insert even a hint of doubt in Alfie's mind. As Alfie idolizes Zack, Beth had thought that perhaps if he talked to her, Alfie might listen.

Zack walks over to the sink line, where Alfie is scrubbing a large pan while humming the melody to "Party in the USA" softly.

Zack taps Alfie on the back.

"Do you have time to take a walk with me over to the lakes?" Zack asks. "There is something which I would like to talk to you about."

Alfie turns around and gives Zack a big smile and a theatrical pose.

"I thought you'd never ask," Alfie says as she removes her ear buds then places the pan at the entrance to the industrial dish washing machine.

Zack walks with Alfie to an area at the rear of the kitchen where the staff changes clothes. Alfie takes off her apron, hair net and rubber boots. She hangs them in half locker numbered 11 and pulls out a pair of silver platform sneakers to go with her khaki-colored culottes and red flower print shirt.

"Now take me away from here, big boy." Alfie says in her best Marlena Dietrich voice, as she links her arm through Zack's and walks out the kitchen exit.

When they have reached the rear exit, Alfie removes her arm and says to Zack, "Sorry about that. They kind of expect a performance from me when I'm leaving the kitchen."

"No need to apologize," Zack says. "Molly tells me that you are thinking of leaving 'The Place'."

"I am," Alfie says as they walk past the rear of 'The Shell' and up the slight incline to the driveway. "I received an offer from the biggest drag bar in Halifax to perform 5 nights a week. It's the kind of opportunity I've been waiting for since forever."

"You are only 17, so forever isn't really a very long time," Zack comments. "Besides you really out to finish up school first."

"Zack," Alfie says turning serious, "tell me what you believe finishing secondary school is going to do for me."

"It might help you get a job," Zack says as they walk across Mountain Way to the paths toward the lake.

"Just what kind of job do you think a queen like me is going to be offered that's better than a promise of being paid $100 a night plus tips to perform?" Alfie asks.

"But what kind of future does that job have?" Zack asks as they approach the first lake.

Two middle aged ladies walk up to Zack and ask for his autograph.

"That's what I'm hoping to find out," Alfie says. "Since I was seven or eight, I knew that I wanted to be a performer. Performing is the only thing which really interests me. Luckily for someone like me, it's also one of the few areas where I might actually have a bit of a chance for a future."

"But isn't seventeen a little young to be on your own?" Zack asks.

"Tell that to the 3 girls at my school, who have gotten themselves knocked up," Alfie says. "Odds are good those girls are headed straight toward a lifetime of emotional train-wrecks, just like my parents. Going to work at Jewel's is an opportunity, not a set of handcuffs."

Zack completes signing the autographs.

"I'm an old 17," Alfie tells Zack. "You'd be surprised how living in the body of the wrong gender makes you grow up fast after you reach puberty."

"Aren't there things which you could learn in school which might help you become a better performer?" Zack asks.

"The things which I need to learn," Alfie says, "aren't taught in public school. I certainly should be able to learn them at Jewel's if I pay attention."

"Have you already outgrown 'Herb's'?" Zack asks in reference to the bar in the village.

"Frankly," Alfie says, "I have. The people who I perform with 2 days a week are high-class amateurs. At this point, I need to learn from professionals. The ladies working at 'Jewel's' are professionals."

A young couple interrupts them to ask Zack for an autograph. He complies before saying to Alfie, "Let's go sit on one of those benches on the other side of the lake".

They walk down the narrow path to the other side of the lake, where currently no one is.

"Alfie," Zack says as they walk, "I'm going to level with you. You have a ton of vocal talent. I really think if that's not your primary focus, you're going to miss out in the long run."

Alfie's penciled in eyebrows raise.

"Thanks for the compliment," she says.

"It's not just a compliment," Zack says. "It's truth. You've got more vocal talent than I ever had. You are a natural entertainer. I only wish that I could play to the audience like you do. I've been talking with Molly about possibly fitting you into my weekend performances after I finish up with this album that I'm doing. I thought maybe we could try out some old Tara Rose songs which Abe and his wife wrote."

Alfie put his hand on Zack's arm, "I really appreciate the offer, but I don't see what singing a couple songs with you is going to do for me. I need this opportunity at Jewel's."

"It will expose you to a whole lot more people," Zack replies.

"Sweetie," Alfie answers, "I think you are overlooking the fact that a whole lot of your audience doesn't want to be exposed to people like me."

"Then they're fools," Zack says angrily.

"The kind of fools, who have kicked my drag queen ass all over Wannasea for most of the past four years," Alfie replies as they reach the bench and sit down.

"Listen," Alfie continues, "I'm really touched that Marie, Beth and you are so concerned about me. It's more concern than my own parents have ever had for me. The thing is that performing at 'Jewel's' is probably the biggest opportunity that I'll have in my life. If I don't grab it, I know I'm going to end up regretting it."

They sit down on the bench. Zack looks silently out across the lake.

"My dream is to become the best drag singer on this planet," Alfie says. "Someday I hope to do that either in London, Berlin, or Paris. Maybe even all three if I can refine my craft. I'm not going to do that by staying in school and messing around down at Herb's or even performing a few duets with you."

"Let me tell you how I ended up where I am at," Zack says suddenly to Alfie.

Zack then spends the next ten minutes going from getting Abby pregnant, being forced out of the Hanover Conservatory, entering the army, and going to Iraq and being injured before starting to work and play in Halifax.

"I used to have drunks throw things at me when I sang over at 'Dave's'," Zack says. "I'm pretty sure that the only reason Dave let me play was because I was a decent bartender and a damned good bouncer. Things can be kind of rough off this island."

Alfie laughs, "Things can be pretty damned rough on this island, too."

"What I'm trying to tell you is that sometimes people tell you one thing because they want you to do something else," Zack says.

"That's a risk which I am fully prepared to take," Alfie replies.

"You know," Zack says more to himself than Alfie, "this just isn't working. I came out here believing that if I talked to you like a responsible adult, it might make you rethink what you are doing. You want to know what I really think?"

"I'm all ears," Alfie says.

"I think that you are probably making the right decision," Zack says. "If being a singer is what you truly believe is your career path, then you need to go for it."

"I'm sure being a drag performer is what I am," Alfie says.

Zack fishes in his jacket pocket and pulls out his cell phone. He swipes it open.

"There is something that you need to promise me," Zack says handing his cell phone to Alfie. "Take my number. When you get over to Halifax, if there is something going on which really bothers you, I want you to call me. If things aren't working out over there, I want you to call me. Will you do that?"

Alfie takes Zack's cell phone and enters the number into his own cell phone, before using his phone to send Zack a message titled "my contact info".

"I'll do that," Alfie says. "Now I want a promise from you. Promise me that you will come over to Halifax and see my act once I get established."

"Deal," Zack replies.

"I'd better get back to the kitchen," Alfie says. "Things were pretty busy over there."

They rise from the bench and walk silently out to the main pathway.

"Are you going to need money or anything to get set up?" Zack asks as they walk back toward the place.

"I'm selling my scooter," Alfie replies, "I've also socked away a $1,400 from my earnings. I think I'll be in good shape."

"Where are you going to live?"

"I'm going to room with two other girls, who perform at 'Jewel's'," Alfie replies. "The guy, who signed me, thinks he can get me a part-time job during the day at one of the large department stores once I get settled if I need it."

"How much will you make from performing?" Zack asks.

"I'll get a hundred a night from the bar," Alfie replies, "but one of the girls, who I will be rooming with, told me she usually makes a couple hundred extra a night from tips."

They walk in silence until reaching the rear of the parking lot to 'the house'.

"I need to run in and see the babies," Zack says, "I've been negligent this week, I haven't seen them since Monday."

Alfie nods his head before gently grabbing hold of Zack's arm and saying, "Thanks, Zack. You don't know what having you on my side means to me."

Alfie disappears around the side of the house headed back to the kitchen.

Zack walks through the parking lot and on to the patio of the house. He sees that Beth is in the studio. He walks to the studio glass door and taps lightly on the glass. Beth, who is standing by the playpen, goes to the door and lets Zack in. Six who has been laying by the door comes to Zack for a head rub.

"Were you able to talk any sense into Alfie?" Beth asks.

Zack walks to the playpen and looks down at the Twins, who are both awake. Julia seems to be working on turning herself over. Nathan is sucking his fingers.

"By taking the job at Jewel's," Zack says to Beth, "Alfie is doing the right thing for her career, maybe it will be her path to stardom. It may be her downfall. I'd suggest that all we can do is make sure that she knows that we are here for her if things fall apart."

Beth is surprised by Zack's statement, but not entirely displeased.

"What are these two guys up to?" Zack asks.

"Julia has learned how to turn herself over," Beth replies. "Nathan is more interested in his fingers and toes."

Fine Tuning

Tuesday, February 11, 10:24AM. Zack is in the SouthTown recording studio control room. He is waiting for Dave. The NorthEnders are inside the studio going over the new song which Zack has asked them to help him record.

Jerome comes in with a copy of sheet music in his hand.

"We think you need to up tempo this a little," Jerome says to Zack.

Zack nugs the sheet from Jerome's hand and looks at it. He takes a minute trying to visual the sound of the song sped up.

"Why don't we try it both ways and see what Dave says?" Zack suggests.

"Sounds okay to me," Jerome replies.

"I hear you guys have a gig at the Caves tomorrow night," Zack comments.

"Yeah," Jerome responds, "if it works out, I think they are going to book us regularly."

"Good deal," Zack says as Jerome goes back into the recording area.

Zack returns to working on the lyrics for another Iraqi Blues song until Dave arrives a few minutes later.

"You guys ready to roll?" Dave asks as he switches on the console and recording equipment.

"Probably as ready as we are ever going to be," Zack says. "We want to try two different tempos. I'd like your opinion on which one sounds better."

"Let's do it," Dave says.

Zack rises from the bench at the console, leaving his tablet in the far corner.

He closes the door behind him as he enters the recording studio.

He walks to the back wall and picks up his electric guitar.

"Let's try your faster version first," Zack says as he heads to his microphone.

After fiddling with tuning for a few minutes, Zack looks out to Dave and nods.

"Take one," Dave says through the audio system.

victim of circumstance 91 BPM *in key of A major in 4/4 time*

    unwanted vision arrives from the past
    producing one helluva blast
    lost in looming wartime trance
    just another victim of circumstance

    cement building quickly crumbles
    through the rubble a survivor stumbles
    five lives gone without a backward glance
    a few more victims of circumstance

    fifteen kids left without parents
    by a guided missile gone errant
    casualties of our advance
    more victims of circumstance

    onward the battle rages
    to where people earn their wages
    despite our moral stance
    twelve more victims of circumstance

    anti-personnel mine explodes
    far from well-traveled roads

caught up in combat's dance
they became victims of circumstance

whoosh of a shoulder fired rocket
headed straight for someone's hip pocket
just part of this war's expanse
claiming one more victim of circumstance

forced to dig their own graves
tyrant responds when one misbehaves
becomes never-ending ghost dance
ever more victims of circumstance

doesn't matter if it's friendly fire
the consequences will still be dire
a future decided by happenstance
just more victims of circumstance

caught up in combat's dance
they became victims of circumstance
casualties of our advance
more victims of circumstance

unwanted memory from the past
produces one helluva blast
lost in a wartime trance
one more victim of circumstance

a future decided by happenstance
just more victims of circumstance
so many lives left to chance
creating more victims of circumstance

all victims of circumstance
we're victims of circumstance
just more victims of circumstance
more victims of circumstance

Zack and the band do the song both ways before Zack sets down his guitar and says, "What do you think, Dave?"

"The first one sounds better to me," Dave replies.

"Play the faster one back for me."

Dave queues the faster version on the audio system. Zack listens to the song carefully.

"The faster one it is," Zack says. "Let's go through it a couple more times.

The band plays the song at the fast pace through twice more before Dave gives the band a thumbs-up gesture.

"The second time through is the keeper," Dave says through the microphone at his console.

As the NorthEnders begin packing up, Zack puts his electric guitar against the back wall and walks back into the control room and sits down. "Two more songs to go," Zack says. "I've put together some lyrics from the next song. Want to see them? "Zack, I need to level with you," Dave says. "I've done a lot of thinking about the offer which you and Molly have made. It's a heck of a deal. I know it would end up making a lot of money for me, but being a songwriter isn't really what I'm cut out to do. What I'm good at is running this board and setting up audio systems. I know decent music when I hear it. I think that I'm pretty good at bringing out the best sounds in decent music. Creating the songs which produce those sounds isn't really my thing."

"You're sure?" Zack asks.

"I'm sure," Dave says. "I hope this won't impact what we've got going on here."

"It won't," Zack says. "I promise you. I'm actually thinking that I should look into buying this building. I've ended up making a lot of money last month. Purchasing this building might be a good place to put it."

Wedding Plans

Wednesday, February 12, 1:34PM. Zack is seated at a picnic table at the far end of the patio at 'The Place'. He's agreed to meet with his mother for lunch. That his mother had called him yesterday and asked to meet for lunch to discuss Saanvi's wedding, caught Zack off-guard. His mother rarely calls him or anyone else.

Prisha arrives at the picnic table along with Judith. Each is carrying a tray. Prisha has two large mugs of Wannasea tea and a plate with a large sandwich. Judith carries a tray with two bowls of vegetable soup and tableware. Prisha sets down the mugs of tea and puts the sandwich in front of Zack.

"Thanks sweetie," Prisha says to Judith after she has placed the soup and cutlery on the picnic table.

As Judith returns to the kitchen, Prisha sits down at the picnic table across from her son.

"Do you like working out here, Mum?" Zack asks.

"Yes," Prisha replies, "though I am a little nervous that I'm going to be on my own starting next week. Sallie is opening her restaurant on Sunday."

"You'll do fine," Zack says. "Everyone is always telling me how much they like working with you."

Zack and his mother eat their food for a few minutes until Zack says, "You said that you'd like to talk about the wedding."

"Saanvi and I came to final agreement on the wedding plans yesterday," Prisha says. "Your sister insists on keeping the ceremony and wedding dinner as simple as possible. It's not what I'd like but it's Saanvi's wedding."

"I've been thinking that I could pay for the wedding and dinner," Zack says before taking a bite from his tuna salad sandwich.

His mother frowns and replies, "That's for your father and I to do."

"Okay," Zack replies hesitantly, "what is it that you'd like from me?"

"Saanvi wants to have a simple Buddhist ceremony," Prisha says. "Will your feelings be hurt if Saanvi does not have you play at the dinner?"

The question catches Zack by surprise. He had assumed since Saanvi announced her engagement that he'd be playing at her wedding. The only question in Zack's mind had been whether he was going to need the NorthEnders to back him up.

"There will be monks chanting," Prisha says. "The ceremony doesn't really lend itself to western music. Saanvi also would make certain that your role at her wedding is as her brother, who can enjoy the ceremony, not as a performer."

"Which means?" Zacks asks knowing there is more behind the statement.

"We would like you to wear a sherwani suit," Prisha says.

"I see," Zack says with a bemused laugh.

Zack has not had on a formal Indian outfit since he was 8. He had rebelled against having to wear the outfit then.

"It will be the same suit which Ray is going to wear," Prisha says.

"Dad?"

"Same suit that you will be wearing," Prisha replies.

Zack now knows why it is his mother making this request rather than Saanvi. This is his mother's idea, being what she'd won from the wedding negotiations with Saanvi. He reaches across the table and takes his mother's hand.

"If it will make you and Saanvi happy," Zack says, "I'll do it. Where am I supposed to get this suit?"

"I'll have a tailor come out and measure you this coming Monday," Prisha says.

Zack spends the next few minutes finishing his lunch.

"What do you think I should get Saanvi and Ray for the wedding?" Zack asks.

"Everyone will be making a small offering after the ceremony to the monks and another for the bride and groom," Prisha replies. "Just put some money in an envelope and place it in the offering."

"I'm thinking maybe $25,000," Zack replies.

"You shall do no such thing, Ralph Jones," Prisha says with her eyes flashing. "That will offend your sister, your father and me. A few hundred will be more than generous."

"But I want to do more," Zack says, "and I can afford to do it."

"You are going to need that money to start your own family someday," Prisha says. "You had better learn to hang on to your money while you have it."

"Aren't Ray and Saanvi buying a house?" Zack replies. "Surely they could use the extra money."

"Your sister has worked very hard," Prisha replies. "She's saved up a very big down payment for their house. She's very proud that she has been able to save enough to make this purchase. Don't make her feel small about it."

"No big shot little brother making a large offering then?" Zack says with a crooked grin.

"If you do it," Prisha says her eyes flashing, "you will have to deal with me."

"Listen mum," Zack says. "I love Saanvi to death. I like Ray. I want to do something for them that they will remember."

"Then just act like Saanvi's very proud brother," Prisha says sipping her tea.

Zack sips on his tea for a few moments as he watches his mother finish her soup.

"Has Saanvi made any plans for the honeymoon?" Zacks asks his mother.

"I think they are planning on using the time to work on their new house," Prisha says.

"I know Saanvi has always wanted to go to Paris," Zack says. "What if I see about setting up an all-expenses paid honeymoon trip to Paris which comes from those working at 'The Place'? I can even see that Beth presents it to Saanvi."

Prisha mulls over Zack's suggestion for a few moments before saying, "Saanvi won't know that you are behind it?"

"I will have Molly handle it," Zack replies. "Saanvi won't know that I had any hand in it except for having made a donation."

Prisha studies her son from a full thirty seconds before replying, "As long as you don't make it a big deal and you are in the background, then yes.'

Zack smiles at his mother and says, "Good deal."

"You know, Prisha says as she sips her tea, "Molly is a very nice girl. She's smart. She's very competent. She really likes you. You should do something about it."

"I know mom," Zack replies. "I really like Molly but I'm not sure that she's the girl for me. Right now, Molly may be the best friend that I have. I don't want to do anything to jeopardize that friendship until I'm sure how I really feel about her."

"It's still that Hanover girl," Prisha says, "isn't it?"

"That Hanover girl" had been how Prisha had referred to Abby for as long as Zack had known Abby.

"Abby is getting married in June," Zack says to his mother.

"So that's going to be when you stop thinking about her and get on with your life?"

Zack mulls the question for a few seconds before replying, "I have gotten on with my life, Mum. The issue is that I'm just not quite certain how I feel about Molly."

"You can lie to yourself, Ralph Jones," Prisha says unflinchingly, "but please don't lie to me."

Gone Flyin

Thursday, February 13, 10:12PM. Zack is in the recording studio at the SouthTown studio working out a slightly different arrangement of 'Six Year Blues' which he wants to put into the Iraqi Blues album.

"Let's try it faster and in the key of F Minor," Zack tells the NorthEnders.

They go through parts of the song, three different times in different tempos, before Zack and the band agree. Zack nods to Dave to begin recording the song. On the second recording, Zack finally seems satisfied with what has been produced.

"Would you play that one back, Dave," Zack says into the microphone.

Dave complies.

"I like it," Zack says. "What do you guys think?"

"Sounds good to me," Clarence says.

Jerome nods his head in agreement.

"You guys ready to try the new one?" Zack asks.

"Give us a few minutes," Jerome replies.

Zack puts down his electric guitar and goes into the control room, while the NorthEnders work out how they will approach the next song.

"You're planning on adding that remix to the new album?" Dave asks.

"Yes," Zack says, "I'm also planning on redoing 'don't blame the alcohol' and 'this side of nowhere. I want to do them using an electric guitar with the guys. I think it will give them a different vibe which fits into this album."

"Should be interesting," Dave says. "Will those songs complete the album?"

"I have one more new song," Zack says. "I'm hoping that it is going to be ready on Sunday. Can you record then?"

"As long as we record in the morning," Dave replies, "I can do it on Sunday. I've got an event to set up out on the east side in the afternoon which begins at 3."

"What time can we start?" Zack asks.

"Nine."

"Works for me," Zack says. "I'll check to make sure that it is okay with the guys."

"We're ready," Jerome says through the studio microphone.

Zack goes back into the recording studio. Closes the door then picks up his electric guitar. After playing a few notes from the first bar, Zack nods to Dave to begin recording.

Flying 72BPM *in the key of C Major in 4/4 time*

> flyin' through the air
> not wanting to be there
> lifted from the ground
> by an operation gone wrong

> when eyes close I go flyin'
> until no tears are left for cryin'
> for the dead or dyin'

> with nothing left to discuss
> it became either them or us
> sent skyward by the blast
> which came from doing what's asked

going flyin' without wings
doesn't work for non-angelic beings
who patrol desert wastelands
fight in' extremist firebrands

when eyes close I go flyin'
until no tears are left for cryin'
for the dead or dyin'

flyin' through the air
not wanting to be there
lifted from the ground
by an operation gone wrong

knowing when I've landed
conscious shall be branded
by doubt, guilt and regret
that I am the one who is left

when eyes close I go flyin'
until no tears are left for cryin'
for the dead or dyin'

rose up' with the explosion
one more part of the commotion
continuing clash of civilizations
bringing more aggravation

just one more bit player
caught on the conveyor
of pushing political will
through a religious gristmill

when eyes close I go flyin' flyin'
until no tears are left for cryin'
for the dead or dyin'

a clash of civilizations
taking place in foreign nations

    with nothing left to discuss
    it becomes either them or us

    going flyin' without wings
    doesn't work for non-angelic beings
    who patrol desert wastelands
    fightin' extremist firebrands

    just another bit player
    caught on the conveyor
    of pushing political will
    through a religious gristmill

    when eyes close I go flyin' flyin'
    until no tears are left for cryin'
    for the dead or dyin'
    I go flyin'

They do the song twice beforeZack asks Dave to play the second recording back. Zack listens to it carefully.

"I think that one works," Zack finally says 30 seconds after the replay has ended. "Are you guys okay with it?"

The band nods their heads.

"Dave?"

"Sounds good to me," Dave says into the control room microphone.

"Do you guys have time to do more?" Zack asks the band.

"I think we can do one more before we have to get back over to the Extension," Jerome says.

"Nowhere or Alcohol," Zack suggests. "Your choice."
"Let's do Nowhere," Clarence replies.

The rest of the NorthEnders nod their agreement.

Over the next forty-five minutes, they do three takes of a slightly modified version of 'This side of nowhere'. Zack and the band decide they like the third recording best.

The Journals

Friday, February 14, 1:44PM. Today is the opening of the Wannasea Historical Society Museum at the Castle. Zack is seated with Ray Simmons at Sam and Sallie's restaurant at the center. The restaurant is almost at full capacity. The pair have just completed eating lunch in preparation for attending Abe's presentation of his grandmother's journals to the society which will include an introduction of future weekly sessions Abe will be giving regarding the contents of those journals.

"We probably should head over to the museum," Ray says as he completes signing the bill.

"Let me run in and tell Sallie how good the meal was," Zack says rising from his chair which is in the first circle of tables looking out through the glass front toward the casino.

"Let Sallie know that I think lunch was terrific," Ray says. "I'm going to give the restaurant a free plug on my podcast tomorrow."

Zack walks around the end of the bar and pops his head into the kitchen, which is alive with activity.

"That meal was terrific," Zack shouts toward Sallie, who is managing the creation of desserts. "I'm going to be telling everyone that they need to come up here and try it out."

"Thanks," Sallie shouts back.

"Ray Simmons says to tell you that it was so good," Zack adds, "that he is going to give you a plug on his podcast."

Sallie gives a thumbs up and calls back, "Tell Abe I wish I could have made his presentation."

"Will do," Zack replies before he meets Ray at the table and walks rapidly across the slate flooring and out the large glass doors of 'Sam & Sallie's'."

They walk around the construction area of the new event center and go into the main entrance of the old Government Center which now serves as the entrance to the museum.

Zack spots Beth standing along the inside wall about twenty feet from the closed entrance doors to museum's main hall.

"Have you met my soon to be brother-in-law?" Zack asks Beth as he walks over to her.

"A few times," Beth says with a smile as she holds out her hand to Ray.

"Beth is one of the people who I interviewed for the articles which I did about you," Ray says as he shakes Beth's hand. "I also spoke to her a number of times about the exposés which I did on Ainsley and Reggie Reginald."

"Isn't Ainsley's trial coming up soon?" Beth says to Ray.

"It is due to start sometime in May," Ray replies.

"Are you going to be covering it?" Beth asks.

"I'm planning on it," Ray replies, "though I haven't received a commitment yet from the Hanover Herald that they will print my coverage of the trial."

"That seems strange,' Beth says, "considering that Valerie Smythe and you were the key reporters on the expose which brought helped to bring Ainsley down."

"Maybe not so odd," Ray replies. "I'm not exactly known for pulling my metaphorical punches. As there are many highly connected people, who are living in fear of what may come out about them if Ainsley makes good on his threat to release his recording, I'm probably not who Herald wants covering Ainsley or the trial for them."

"Certainly, sounds as though that trial will be quite the show," Beth says.

"No matter what the Herald does," Ray states, "I'm going to cover the trial. I'm also planning on continuing to dig into Ainsley's past. I'm now thinking that there may be a book in it."

"I'd certainly be interested in that kind of book," Beth says.

"If I write one," Ray says, "I promise that I will send you a signed first copy."

The doors to the main hall swing open. The main hall, which the Reginald's had used as their meeting room, is dark and imposing. The stone walls are covered with battle flags and large paintings of Beth and Abe's Reginald ancestors. The room is also somewhat chilly despite a fire which is roaring in the fireplace along the south wall of the hall.

Beth, Ray, and Zack file into the room along with about thirty other people. They take seats in the third row. Abe, who is holding a large folio, is seated on a small dais at the rear of the large hall next to Steve DeJean. By 2PM, approximately fifty people are seated in folding chairs in the large hall.

Steve DeJean rises and walks to a small podium with a microphone in the center of the dais.

"Good afternoon, everyone," Steve DeJean says. "It is my great pleasure to welcome you to a Wannasea Island historical artifact donation ceremony on this first day of the Wannasea Historical Society Museum being open. Abraham Stolz, noted Wannasea Island innkeeper, songwriter, and historian, will be presenting the museum with three journals which belonged to his maternal grandmother, Alice Bailey Reginald. Before Abe presents us with the journals, I would like him to tell you a little bit about the journals and their discovery."

Abe rises from his chair to polite applause. After exchanging a handshake with DeJean, Abe walks to the podium.

"Good afternoon," Abe begins. "The three journals which I will be presenting to the museum were discovered to be in the false bottom of a large chest which was in my mother's possession for the better part of sixty years. The chest is something which was passed along to my mother, after Alice Bailey's death. I have no reason to believe that my mother had any idea that the chest contained a false bottom or the journals. Writings in the journals cover a period from 1691 to 1913. Little of the content of the journals was written by Alice Bailey. The journals cover much of the history of our island from its settlement through the beginning of what we have been calling 'the fall of the Reginalds'. What I have learned from the journals is that much of that history of this island, which we have been taught, is incorrect. Beginning next Wednesday, I will have weekly forty-minute sessions in this hall which outline the contents of the journals starting with the earliest entries and their impact upon our island's history.

In a blatant attempt to tease interest in those sessions, I will share with you a few entries in the journals. Here is one from 11 June 1788:

"That cockalorum Nieddo has struck once more. The fools on the hill have brought the French down on us with no apparent regard for thee or thine. Nieddo's boastful ways have become our ruin. Fleeing the island may be our only relief."

A cockalorum is a little person with an extremely high opinion of themselves. Nieddo is the actual familial name of the Reginalds. The name came from Corsica. In April of 1788, the French had lost a ship off the west end of our island during a hurricane.

The Reginalds found some valuable flotsam from the wreckage of the ship. The Reginalds had been going around the island bragging that they had taken the French ship down when the reality is all they had done was quickly looted the wreck site. The French heard of the Reginald's bragging and threatened havoc on the islanders for the better part of four months while the Reginalds hid in South Island caves. What the Reginalds managed to salvage from that French ship is what eventually enabled them to buy property on this mountain where this museum now sits. The islanders were so put off by these actions on the part of the Reginalds that they basically remained at war with them for the next 25 years.

Here is another entry from 6 February 1911. I believe this entry was written by Alice Bailey's cousin Merle.

"Hugo brings greetings from Naval Intelligence Department. Hugo says WIPA must scuttle every deal Theo has made. Stifle the scoundrel at every turn. We must be willing to put down the knife and fork in order to give dear Theo an earth bath. It is the only way."

What makes this entry interesting is that I was taught that Alice Bailey brought Hugo into the WIPA. Alice had no role in WIPA in 1911. Based upon other entries in the third journal, I have discovered that Hugo believed his father to be responsible for his mother's early death. Hugo was also instrumental in the creation and expansion of the Wannasea Island Protection Association (WIPA) from 1908 onward. Hugo was working to bring down the Reginalds at least four years before Alice and her cousins, Hugo helped plot his brother's demise. With help from Mainland Intelligence Services, Hugo, Alice, and other islanders were able to pull it off. In Hugo's defense, his brother Theo had a long-standing history of murderous psychopathic behavior.

These journals have led me to believe that Hugo, not Alice, was the original revolutionary. Perhaps more subversive than revolutionary, for his primary driver for wanting to take down his father was to avenge his mother. Just as Alice was interested in bringing down Theo to protect her cousins, as well as herself. Democracy was a secondary consideration driven in large part by the Reginalds constantly bringing malicious forces on to the island in failed attempts to expand their influence. What the journals do not make clear is why the falsehood was pushed that it was Alice, who brought Hugo into the rebellion.

Additionally, I have learned from the journals that the only people on this island, ever recognizing the Nieddo cum Reginalds as their rulers were the Nieddos themselves. The rest of the island saw them as an aggravating annoyance. This very castle was a monument which the last two Reginalds built to themselves, not for the governance of the island. Prior to the formation of Wannasea Island democracy, the closest thing to governing which took place here was the Reginalds trying to figure out how they could squeeze more money out of the islanders in return for their water. The only real governance of the island was done by the Wannasea Alliance until Hugo turned this castle over to the island. What I have been able to decipher from the journals outlines this very clearly.

Before turning the journals over to the Historical Society, I want to express a deep debt of gratitude to my assistant, Ms. Molly Peters, who put in so much hard work copying and transcribing the journals. Over the next few months, we will be providing copies of the journals on the Wannasea Historical Society Museum website. Much of the journals are written in foreign languages such as Romanian, Greek, and Latin. Some of the writings in the journals have not yet been deciphered. Think of Molly and thank her when you access that information."

Abe walks back to his chair and picks up the folio from atop it. He pulls the aged, leather-bound journals from the folio. With Steve DeJean trailing him, Abe returns to the podium.

"I would now like to bequeath these journals to the Wannasea Historical Society Museum for perpetuity," Abe says as he hands the journals over to Steve DeJean.

End Of Production

Sunday, February 15, 9:12PM. Zack and the NorthEnders have just completed their first run through the final song which Zack is planning on doing for his Iraqi Blues album.

"I think we ought to try it just a little slower," Zack says to the band.

The band tries different tempo over the next ten minutes before Zack says, "Let's go with that one."

Zack nods to Dave, who begins recording.

what more   76 BPM in key of F Major in 4/4 time

desert sun burns so hot
must be part of fedayeen plot
to sap our strength
and give this battle length

three days without sleep
we've gotten ourselves in deep
no way forward, no way back
just another stalled attack

die or live
what more
can we give

staring across the empty space
to where Mookie's guns are placed
Basra's not a welcoming town
when what passed for peace runs aground

nothing in this war is ever determinative
each doing to the other what neither will forgive
enough to make any sane person shout
until the powers-that-be decide to pull out

    die or live
    what more
    can we give

  soon a truce will be arranged
 serious grievances remain unchanged
both sides claiming victory for a tie score
 another fruitless battle in an endless war

    die or live
    what more
    can we give

 enough to make any sane person shout
until the powers-that-be decide to pull out
both sides claiming victory for a tie score
 another fruitless battle of an endless war

    die or live
    what more
    can we give

 nothing in this war ever determinative
each doing to the other what neither will forgive
 enough to make any sane person shout
 until the powers-that-be decide to pull out

    die or live
    what more
    can we give

    die or live
    what more
    can we give

They do the song three more times before Zack is satisfied.

"I'm going to go out and see what Dave and Molly think," Zack says putting down his electric guitar and walking out of recording studio door.

Molly is seated in a desk chair behind Dave working on her tablet.

"Do you guys like that last take?" Zack asks.

"Seems like the best one to me,' Dave says, "Do you want me to play it back?"

"Please," Zack says as he sets down on the console bench to listen to the replay of the last recording.

Zack nods his head as the replay ends.

"That's the one as far as I am concerned," Zack says. "Molly, what do you think?"

"Seems okay to me," Molly says. "Are you guys going to have time to record the album introduction today?"

"How long is it?" Dave asks.

"It's two paragraphs," Molly replies. "It probably won't be more 2 minutes."

"We should have time," Dave says. "As long as we don't have to do too many cuts."

"Let's get the remix of 'Alcohol' in first," Zack says as he rises and begins walking into the studio.

"You guys ready?" Zack asks as he closes the door behind him.

The Northenders nod their heads.

Two takes of a slightly slower, more bassy electric version of 'Don't Blame it on the Alcohol' are recorded.

"What do you guys think?" Zack asks.

"I like it better than the recording that's currently on the website," Jerome says. "It's almost as if they are two different songs."

"We're going to leave the old recording up on our website," Zack says, "this one will go in the album and only be for sale through our music distribution channel."

Zack walks out of the recording studio into the control room.

"That second one is a keeper," Dave says. "Guess that is a wrap on your album."

"Other than the introduction," Molly interjects.

Zack turns and pops his head into the recording studio door.

"That's a wrap guys," Zack says. "Thanks a million for your work to reach this point."

The NorthEnders begin packing up as Zack goes back into the control room and walks up to Molly.

"What do you have?" Zack asks Molly.

Molly hands him her tablet which has a two-paragraph introduction which she has created for Zack to record as the opening to the album.

"Are you okay if I contact the people at the Hanover Medical facility now to arrange setting up the concert there?" Molly asks.

"Sure," Zack says.

"Any particular date you'd like to do it?" Molly asks.

"Either on a Sunday or Thursday night," Zack replies. "I'd like at least a couple weeks to decompress if you can arrange it."

"How about Sunday, March 16th?" Molly suggests.

"Sounds good to me," Zack says. "Do you mind if I change this introduction around a little?" Zack and Molly go back and forth for the next five minutes on the introduction before they reach agreement.

Zack returns to the now empty recording studio, closing the door behind him before walking to the main microphone with Molly's tablet in his hand.

Zack nods to Dave before saying into the microphone, "Hi everyone. This is Zack Tillerman. I've made this introduction to our new album, Iraqi Blues, to explain not only why this album is a departure from what you have heard from us before, but to give you a little background to the source for most of the songs on this album."

Zack pauses for a brief second before continuing, "In the years 2008 and 2009, I spent 8 months in Iraq as a forward scout for an APV unit. On December 8th, the APV in which I'd been riding was blown apart by an IED. Clint Chadwick, the APV pilot and Hiram Williams, the gunner, were killed in that explosion. I was injured by the blast and spent fourteen months in the Hanover Medical Facility recovering from wounds. There are not many times when I close my eyes that I don't go back to riding in that APV with Clint and Hi. Clint taught me to play guitar. Hi taught me not to take myself so damned seriously. I still am unable to understand why I am still here, and they are gone."

Zack pauses again for a brief moment.

"Originally, I wanted to call this album 'The Big Suck Blues'. My partners talked me out of it. Those of you, who have done the "Big Suck', know exactly why I wanted that name for this album. The songs on this album are for all the men and women, who have given so much of themselves in Iraq and other wars. Wars, most of which, have resulted in an undetermined and confusing outcome. You will always and forever be my mates."

Zack backs away from the microphone. Dave ends the recording.

Moving On

Tuesday, February 18, 10:19AM. Zack has his battered and beaten VW Bug headed up Mountain Way to Mountain Village for a meeting with Molly about how to proceed with the release of the Iraqi Blues album and the scheduling of a concert at Hanover Medical Facility.

Zack swings his vehicle up the driveway toward the Rebecca Stolz Meeting Center.

Molly has been pressuring Zack to do something about creating a press statement about the release of the album. Yesterday Zack worked with Dave to put up an announcement about the album on the website. Zack is hoping what they have put on the website will appease Molly.

Zack pulls into the parking lot for Mountain Village. The lot is approximately 2/3rds full. He jumps out of the Beetle and walks across the lot into the center. Annette is at the main counter for the facility.

"Hey stranger," Annette says to Zack. "Haven't seen you around here for a few weeks."

"We've been tied up down in SouthTown finishing up the album," Zack says. "How are things going with you."

"Good," Annette replies. "We are finally getting into a routine here and at 'The Shell'."

"Routines can be good," Zack says. "Is Molly around?"

"She's up in the little conference room,' Annette replies. "Do you want me to call her."

"I think I remember where it is at," Zack says as he turns from the counter and heads toward the stairs. "See you later."

Zack climbs the stairs, turns left, and goes to the small conference room at the back of the hallway. Molly is seated at the conference room table. Zack pulls his tablet out of the large inside pocket of his windbreaker.

"Hanover wants to know if you mind if they livestream your concert on the Military Broadcast Network," Molly says as Zack takes a seat across from her.

"That's okay with me," Zack says disinterestedly.

"Are you planning on having Dave record the concert?" Molly asks.

"Hadn't thought about it," Zack says. "Maybe Dave can work with the Military Broadcast team, and they will provide us with a copy of their recording?"

"I'll ask them about it," Molly says. "I already told them that we will only give them rights to broadcast the concert live. Any recordings of the concert belong to us."

"Okay," Zack replies knowing Molly can be a hard ass when she wants to be. "Have they verified March 16 as the date for the concert?"

"They have," Molly says. "They are going to set up a facility on their parade grounds. They are projecting as many as 5,000 people may attend."

"As long as most of the people are servicemembers or medical staff," Zack replies, "I'm good with that."

"What have Dave and you come up with regarding a press release?" Molly asks.

Zack turns on his tablet, logs in and goes to the ZackTillerman.com website. He shows Molly the announcement which Dave and he have put together. It reads, "Zack Tillerman is pleased to announce the release of a new album entitled "Iraqi Blues". The album is something of a departure from what you may have come to expect from us. We feel that it is a slightly different form of traditional blues. The album was influenced by time spent in Iraq. This album is dedicated to those who have served in Iraq and elsewhere. The album is available only from the ZackTillerman music distribution service."

Below the blurb is a link to the music distribution channel.

"I think that should work for general release," Molly says. "I've contacted a few reporters, who have written articles about you either in the recording industry media or for the entertainment portions of bigger newspapers. Three of them have indicated they want to come out and interview you next week." "Can't we do it when I'm over in Hanover?" Zack asks.

"No," Molly replies. "They want to have their articles ready to be published on March 15th. That doesn't give them enough time to have them ready. I've set up the interviews for Monday, Tuesday, and Thursday of next week."

"Where are these interviews going to occur?" Zack asks.

"Here and down at 'The Place'," Molly replies. "None of the interviews should last longer than a couple hours."

Zack knows that it is a waste of time to argue with Molly about the interviews.

"I think we need to hire a publicist," Molly says as she slides Zack's tablet back to him.

"Why don't we just wait and see where we are a week or so after we have the concert?" Zack asks.

"Because there is this thing called striking while the iron is hot," Molly replies.

"I'm of the opinion that we won't know if the iron is hot until a week or so after we do the concert," Zack replies. "We also have this issue of not really knowing where our LLC stands since Dave decided that he doesn't want to come in with us."

"I'm not sure I see what one has to do with other," Molly says.

"If the album fizzles and goes nowhere," Zack counters, "we'll know that we may need to hire more than a publicist to get us back on track. If the album takes off, we are going to have other kinds of worries and will need other kinds of people."

"That actually makes sense," Molly responds. "Sometimes you can actually surprise me."

"I'm not a total noob," Zack says with a sarcastic grin.

"I'm willing to wait until the end of March to see where we stand," Molly says. "After that we are going to have to do something. Either get a manager and publicist or an agent or some type of management service like that guy from Mainland Talent Agency presented."

"Let's wait and see," Zack says.

Molly frowns. She knows that 'wait and see' is Zack's way of not addressing something which he doesn't want to address.

Molly pulls out five printed sheets which contain the latest financial statement for ZackTillerman LLC. She hands them to Zack who looks them over without a great deal of interest.

"Olivia called me and said that Abe would now like to be out of the LLC formally on March 1st," Molly says. "That's next Thursday. I've also been speaking with Abe's agent about how to deal with proceeds from this songwriting library."

Zack whistles loudly as he reads the final print out.

"That's a lot of money," Zack says pointing to the $428,559.61 net profit figure at bottom of the final sheet which Molly handed him.

"It could be a lot more, if we started doing this more professionally."

Zack grimaces and reaches his hand across the conference room table and places it on top of Molly's hand.

"Molly," Zack says peering directly into the bright blue eyes behind her glasses, "I really appreciate all the stuff which you are doing. I'd be lost without you. The problem is that I'm really not all that interested in dealing with any of this, right now, All I can seem to think about right now is decompressing."

"You're patronizing me," Molly says sliding her hand out from under Zack's.

"I don't think you understand how much making these 'Big Suck Blues' has taken out of me," Zack rejoins.

"I do understand," Molly counters. "It's why I keep suggesting that we need help."

Incidental Contact

Sunday, February 23, 9:34AM. After having just completed his workout, Zack is seated upon a folding beach chair in front of a large beach towel at Southwest Beach. The beach is relatively uncrowded. Zack's cell phone rings. He pulls it out of the rucksack which is laying on the towel.

"Ralph Jones," Zack answers the phone.

"Ralph, this is Royce Toles," Zack hears through the speaker.

Royce Toles is the owner of the building in SouthTown which Zack and Dave use as a recording studio.

"I've given some thought to your offer to purchase the old drug store building which I currently rent to you," Toles says. "If you'd be willing to pay me $275 thousand for it, I'm willing to sell it to you."

Zack and Dave currently have a two-year lease on the building. They have put quite a bit of work into the recording studio and control room. Zack thinks that price may be slightly more than the building is actually worth.

"How about $260 thousand?" Zack asks.

"That's tempting," Toles replies, "but it seems a little low. Can you do 265?"

Although that price still seems a little high to Zack, Zack decides he doesn't want to dicker further. Zack and Dave want to put more money into the recording studio but can't see doing that if someone else owns the building.

"I'll do $265,000," Zacks responds.

As Zack says this, his eyes are drawn to two figures coming toward him from the west about 75 yards away. One of those figures looks very much like Abby.

"I'll have my lawyer draw up a contract and work out getting all the appropriate documents and approvals put together," Toles says. "I'm assuming this deal is going to be cash as you said."

"Yes," Zack replies as his eyes remain focused on the figure coming toward him, "it will be a cash deal."

"I'll call you back when I've got everything together," Toles responds.

"Talk with you then," Zack says before disconnecting the call and putting the cell phone into the pocket of his swim trunks.

Zack turns and watches the two women walk toward him. The one. who he thinks is Abby, has on a thin peach beach wrap covering a bright orange two-piece swimsuit. The other woman, who has bright red hair has on a silver beach wrap covering a burgundy swimsuit. The closer the women are, the more certain Zack is that it is Abby. She is flashing a big smile.

"Didn't think we'd find you out here," Abby says as she gets within 25 feet of him.

Despite how uncomfortable her presence makes him, Zack smiles back at Abby.

"I'm usually out here a little earlier in the morning," Zack replies. "I'm running a little late today."

"Katy," Abby says turning to the redhead, "this is RJ. He and I played in a string quartet in secondary school."

Zack extends his hand to the redhead, who gives him a quizzical smile, before shaking his hand.

"RJ," Abby continues, "this is Katy McConnell. Katy and I play together in a string ensemble at Coventry. Katy plays the viola."

"Nice to meet you," Zack says to the redhead.

"Don't you go by Zack Tillerman now?" Katy asks.

"When I'm performing," Zack says. "Otherwise, just I have always done, I respond to any name that anyone chooses to call me."

"I see," Katy says. "Should I call you RJ or Zack?"

"Your choice," Zack replies flashing an impish grin.

"I like Zack better," Katy says with a smile. "I saw that you put out a new album earlier this week, how is that going?"

"To be honest," Zack replies, "I really haven't paid too much attention to it. We are going to formally launch the album at the Hanover Medical Center in the middle of next month. Until then, I'm taking a little hiatus from music writing."

"You aren't playing at 'The Place'?" Abby asks.

"That's all that I'm doing," Zack replies. "It's kind of like taking a vacation."

"I've heard a couple of your songs," Katy says. "They really are quite remarkable."

"Is that good or bad?" Zack asks.

"I'm not much of a blues person," Katy replies, "but those songs seem to reach out and grab hold of you. I can only imagine how someone who went through Iraq might feel about them."

"Guess we'll find out on the 16th of March," Zack replies. "What brings you out to the island?"

"We decided that we needed to chill a little," Abby says. "School is starting to drag on us right now."

Zack chooses to remain silent. Standing this near to Abby isn't doing his mind any good.

"We are going to walk down to the islands," Katy says. "Want to join us?"

"Sorry," Zack lies, "I've got a brunch date in SouthTown. Would you mind if I talk to Abby for a minute or two in private?"

"Of course not," Katy says before turning to Abby and saying, "I'll walk really slow, you can catch up with me when you are finished."

Zack waits until Katy has gone a good fifteen yards before turning to Abby and saying somewhat gruffly, "What are you doing?"

"Some of your new music has me worried," Abby says sheepishly. "I wanted to see for myself how you are getting along but honestly, I wasn't sure that I would run into you."

"You enjoy torturing me?" Zack replies softly.

Abby puts her hand on Zack's arm. Hurt creeps into her eyes.

"Seeing me is now torture?" Abby asks.

"In a manner of speaking, it certainly is," Zack replies with downcast eyes.

"I care about you, RJ," Abby says. "I cannot stop myself from caring about you."

"If you care about me," Zack replies, "you'll stay away from me until you have your feelings sorted out."

"I think that I do have my feelings sorted out," Abby replies. "I care very much what happens to you."

"Are you still engaged?" Zack asks.

"Yes," Abby says, "I don't think that the two are mutually exclusive."

"I'm here to tell you that they are," Zack says.

"That album you just put out frightens me," Abby says. "It's dark. I worry that your life has become filled with darkness."

"Serving in a war zone is dark," Zack says, "Part of that darkness is always going to be with me, but it's a darkness with which I'm learning how to deal. That was the main point of making the album."

"Some of those songs still make me worried for you," Abby says.

"Then for your own sake," Zack says a little too aggressively, "don't listen to them."

Abby squeezes Zack's arm, "Don't cut me out of your life."

"You can't have it both ways, Abby," Zack says hotly. "Either you've moved past me, or you haven't."

Tears coming into Abby's eyes, "Don't do this to me, RJ."

"You are doing it to yourself," Zack replies.

"You really don't want to see me anymore?" Abby says hesitantly.

"I don't want to see you until you've sorted yourself out," Zack says. "That means either you are going through with this wedding and putting me completely out of your life, or you are going to break off your engagement and the two of us can figure out where we stand."

"I'm not sure that I'm strong enough to make that choice just yet," Abby says.

"You are going to have to be," Zack replies. "I need you to promise me that until you know where you stand that you will stay away from me and stop sending your friends out on scouting trips to find out how I'm doing."

Abby looks at Zack with pleading eyes.

Abby moves close to Zack and tightens her grip on Zack's arm.

"You need to promise me," Zack says forcing himself to look away from Abby's eyes.

Abby leans over and places a kiss on Zack's cheek, then begins walking away from him.

"I promise," Abby says without turning around to look at Zack.

Questions

Tuesday, February 25, 2:12AM. Zack is standing on the front of the stage at 'The Place'. He has one hip on the stool. He is looking out into an empty dining room as a photographer from the MainLand Scene takes pictures of him. The reporter, who is interviewing him, is sitting at a table on the bar side of the front row.

Yesterday, Zack was interviewed by a reporter from the Vibe. That interview and photo session was something of a fluff piece. Jeremy Wade, the reporter from the Scene, appears to be a different sort.

"I've got enough," the photographer tells Zack.

Zack rises from the stool and walks back to the table where Wade sits in front of two steaming cups of coffee which Molly has just brought. Molly then goes back to the bar area and has seated herself behind the stool at the cash register. Her eyes and ears remain focused on the reporter.

"I know that your given name is Ralph Jones," Wade says to Zack. "How did you get the stage name of Zack Tillerman?"

"A few years back, when I was interviewing to play here, Abe Stolz gave me the name. My father used to play here in a folk band called 'The Tillers'. Abe thought the name Tillerman suited me."

"Where did the Zack come from?" Wade asks.

"Out of Abe's head."

"Abe Stolz is who you write songs with," Wade responds, "isn't he?"

"Wrote songs with," Zack corrects. "Abe retired from songwriting last month."

"Am I correct in saying Abe Stolz has become too old to write songs any longer?" Wade interjects.

The question raises Zacks hackles and shows in his reply. "Most of the songs which I have released, have lyrics created by Abe," Zack replies. "Abe Stolz has been associated with 'The Place' for over 60 years. I don't think of Abe as some old guy. Most people around here think of Abe as 'the Sage of Wannasea Mountain'."

"Why do you still choose to play in small venue like this," Wade beings, "when you could be playing in much larger venues on the Mainland or on the Continent?"

"Big crowds don't interest me," Zack replies. "I feel comfortable playing here. Playing in a smaller venue gives me a much better appreciation for both the music and my audience."

"You now play here on Wednesday, Friday and Saturday?" Wade asks.

"On Wednesday night, we do sea and folk songs inside," Zack replies. "On Friday and Saturday, I do blues and folk rock out in 'The Shell'."

At the start of today's interview, Wade had toured 'The Shell'. He had pictures taken of Zack standing in front of the stage. "Why do you still bother playing sea and folk songs?" Wade inquires.

"I grew up listening to and playing sea and folk songs. I honestly enjoy folk and sea songs the most. Playing them here on Wednesday nights has become a relief valve for me. Those Wednesday performances keep me grounded. They reminded where I come from and why I enjoy playing music."

"So commercial success isn't high on your list of goals?" Wade suggests.

"No, it is not," Zack replies. "I'm more interested in having fun playing and making music in the hope that my audience will enjoy what I put out."

"I wouldn't exactly call this latest album of yours, 'Iraqi Blues', fun," Wade states. "It's one of the darker albums which I've come across in recent years."

"'Iraqi Blues' was meant to be different," Zack replies. "It something of a musical primal scream and meant to cathartic. Both for me and those who hear it."

"Cathartic or not," Wade says, "that album is on fire. The last time that I checked, I believe that you've sold almost a half a million copies of it."

This statement catches Zack off-guard. Zack has paid no attention to how well 'Iraqi Blues' is selling. He had gotten Molly to agree not to bother him with sales figures or anything else related to the album until the Wednesday before the Hanover concert.

"Molly," Zack calls over the coffee bar, "how many copies of 'Iraqi Blues' have been sold?"

Molly lifts her tablet from the counter by the cash register and uses it to access the website for their music distribution channel.

"547,323 as of noon," Molly replies. "Interestingly many of those sales are coming from beyond the MainLand. The North America sales figure is over 300K."

Zack is stunned by Molly's statement.

"You don't mean to tell me that you had no idea how many copies of your new albums have been sold until just a moment ago?" Wade says looking at Zack contemptuously.

Zack shrugs his shoulders and says nothing.

"Do you have any tours lined up?" Wade asks.

"Outside of the March 16th concert at the Hanover Medical Facility," Zack says, "I have no plans to play any other venue than here."

Wade shakes his head.

"I've been told that a love affair gone wrong is why you enlisted in the Army," Wade states. "Is that accurate?"

Zack wonders who told Wade this information.

"No, that's not correct," Zack replies. "I come from a lower middle-class family, who could not afford to send me to the university. After secondary school, I did what many people my age do when they have trouble finding steady employment, I went into the military."

"I have been told that you were an accomplished cello player," Wade rejoins. "Weren't you on track to go to the Hanover Conservatory for graduate studies."

"Plenty of people are on track to do things," Zack replies. "I got off-track in my last year of secondary school. Hanover Conservatory no longer had any interest in me. There wasn't much left for me to do but go into the military."

"What instruments do you play?" Wade asks.

"The violin was where I started," Zack replies. "My dad taught me to play. I moved on to viola and cello from there. I didn't pick up the guitar until I was in Iraq."

"Allegedly one of your tracked vehicle crew members taught you to play guitar," Wade says.

"Clint Chadwick, the pilot of our APV, taught me guitar basics," Zack responds.

"Was this Chadwick a good guitar player?" Wade asks.

Zack smiles before responding, "Clint was a good teacher. Once he had shown me everything that he knew, I used instruction courses on the internet to go further."

"How long were you with Chadwick?" Wade asks.

"Slightly more than eight months," Zack replies.

"How did you come to be in this particular tracked vehicle crew?" Wade inquires.

Zack smiles again.

"When I was first in Iraq, I was assigned to another crew. The members of that crew didn't like it that I looked so much like an Iraqi. They did what they could to get rid of me. Clint has already started teaching me guitar, so he knew me. Two bottles of Laiphroaig 25 moved me over to Chadwick and Williams's vehicle."

"They were both killed by an explosive device eight months later," Wade states. "Correct?"

Zack nods his head.

"Would you care to talk about that incident?" Wade asks.

"Not really," Zack says. "Anyone, who is interested, can listen to 'Iraqi Blues' to understand what happened."

"You were wounded in that incident, weren't you?"

Zack nods his head.

"What were your injuries?" Wade asks.

Zack is growing weary of this interview.

"As many of the people at the Hanover Medical Facility used to say, "I got my ass shot off"."

"Do you have any lasting disabilities from it?" Wade asks.

"We all have disabilities," Zack replies. "Mine just aren't quite as easy to spot."

Wade clicks off his recording device and says, "I think that about wraps it up. Would you mind walking out to the parking lot with me. I'd like our photographer to get a few photos of you standing next to that Volkswagen of yours."

Needs

Sunday, March 9, 12:04AM. Zack has fallen asleep in the armchair in the backstage area of 'the Shell'. Over the past few weeks, he has gotten into the habit of waiting until the crowds clear out before leaving the facility after his performance. Zack will sit in the chair and catch up on his messages or pull out his tablet and write down lines which have the potential to be turned into new songs.

Molly unlocks the outside door and enters the dimly lit backstage area. After her eyes adjust to the change in lighting, she sees Zack sleeping in the chair. As she begins walking toward him, Zack is startled awake.

Molly sees the anxiety which is alive in Zack eyes as he jumps up from the chair.

'He's just come back from Iraq again,' Molly thinks as she watches Zack get his bearings.

"I didn't mean to startle you," Molly says.

'That's okay," Zack says as he shakes himself awake. "I should have been out of here an hour ago."

"I saw your car parked behind the Meeting Center when I was walking over to my place," Molly replies, "and got a little worried about what had happened to you."

"I'm good," Zack replies, "just haven't been getting as much sleep as I should lately."

Zack pulls on his jacket, which was over the back of the armchair, and places his tablet, which is still in hist right hand, in its inside pocket. He walks toward the exit and follows Molly out the side door.

"It was a really good show, tonight" Molly says. "The crowd was really into it."

"Thanks," Zack says as he walks up beside Molly.

Molly places her arm inside of Zack's right arm.

"Do you think," Molly suggests, "that you should continue holding off on playing the new 'Iraqi Blues' songs. The crowd really wanted to hear them tonight."

"The first time that I'm going to do them will be over in Hanover," Zack says stubbornly. "There will be plenty of time for people to hear me play them after that concert."

"A lot of those people, who came to see you tonight, may very likely never get to see you play live again," Molly says. "Marie was just explaining to me how hard it is to get tickets to your performances now. She says that she is having a heck of time preventing ticket scalpers from gobbling up all the tickets for future events."

"Hadn't thought of that," Zack says. "Maybe I ought to consider doing some unscheduled free performances after the Hanover concert? I've been thinking it might be nice to have a big outside concert down at Southwest Beach when it warms up."

"That sounds like an option," Molly says.

They walk about twenty yards uphill toward the Meeting Center. Zack has taken to parking his car there when he goes to his performances at 'the Place'. His battered VW has become too big a magnet for fans.

"Want to come to my place?" Molly asks. "I'll make you a really nice drink."

Despite his promise to himself to try to uncomplicate his life, Zack says, "I'd like that."

They walk past the rear loading area, where Zack's battered VW Beetle sits, past the Meeting Center and across the parking lot. The night is still and clear. The star constellations of Taurus and Gemini shine in the dark sky.

The lights of Molly's unit flash on as they come to her deck. Molly enters her security code to unlock the sliding glass door.

"In the event that you are interested," Molly says to Zack, "my code is the last 6 digits of my cell phone number."

Zack decides not to say that he really isn't all that interested in knowing the code to Molly's unit.

Molly waits for Zack to hand her his jacket.

"You know the drill," Molly says as she hangs Zack's jacket up on the inside hook attached to her left-side closet.

Zack walks to the couch in the rear of the units and plops down. He decides against turning on Molly's tv.

"I've got two kinds of rum," Molly says, "or some red or white wine."

"Rum," Zack says.

"Rum and coke or I can do a mojito, if you'd like?"

"I'll try the mojito," Zack replies.

Molly begins getting out the ingredients to make mojitos.

"Have you heard anything back from Toles yet?" Molly asks referring to Zack's plan to buy the building in SouthTown which they are using as a recording studio.

"He says that the paperwork should be ready the week of March 24th," Zack replies.

"You know," Molly replies, "you really should have Olivia look over all that stuff."

"That's probably a good idea," Zack says.

"If you want, I'll call Olivia on Monday and arrange for her to take a look at them."

"That would be good," Zack says while suppressing a yawn.

Molly comes to the couch and hands a mojito to Zack. She sits down on the couch as close to Zack as possible with the other mojito in her right hand. Zack takes a generous sip of the drink.

"Wow," Zack says delightedly, "that's a damned good drink. I think if this business management thing doesn't work out for you, you could have a terrific future as a bartender."

"I'll stick to finance, thank you."

"I'm not just saying this drink is good to be nice," Zack says. "I used to be a bartender; you know."

"The story I heard was that Dave's liked having you work over there because you were the only bouncer around, who could handle all of the drunks hanging out in that place," Molly says with a laugh.

"Who told you this?"

"I've got my sources," Molly replies as she wiggles herself even closer to Zack, "and I refuse to reveal them unless you threaten me with bodily harm."

Zack smiles despite himself.

"You have a ridiculous amount of money coming in this month," Molly says as she takes a sip of her drink.

Zack decides to overlook that Molly had promised not to talk to him about album sales until after the 20th.

"How much?" Zack asks.

"At least three million," Molly replies.

Zack raises his eyebrows before taking another sip of his drink.

"You really need to think about investing that money somewhere," Molly says. "You should create a cushion to fall back upon if your career stalls or something happens."

Zack laughs, "So you brought me here to liquor me up and seduce me into making investments?"

"I like the seduce part," Molly says, "but I'm not actually thinking cash investments."

Molly takes Zack's hand and places it in her lap.

"I think you're right," Zack says somewhat nervously. "I really should be putting aside some of that money. Why don't we start by putting me on a budget after I get this deal done on the recording studio?"

Molly wriggles her chest against Zack's left shoulder as she moves a little sideways and takes another sip of her drink.

"How much do you think you need to live on?" Molly asks.

"I can get by on $2,000 per month," Zack says as he carefully inches himself away.

"What do you want to invest in?" Molly asks.

"Something secure," Zack says. "Something which will keep up with inflation and be there if I need it."

"I'm invested in a couple different funds through the Farmer's Union Bank," Molly says. "They do okay. Do you want me to see if the bank will set something up for you?"

"Sure," Zack says after he finishes the rest of his drink.

"Want another one?" Molly asks, taking the empty glass from Zack's hand.

"Nah," Zack replies, "I've got to be up in a few hours to do my workout down at the beach. If I don't get my workout in before 8Am, all that I will get done at the beach is signing autographs."

"Why don't you stay here with me?" Molly asks as she reclaims the last little bit of space Zack had managed to create between them.

"Molly," Zack says, "we've been over this. Until I get my life in order, I'm not about to risk damaging you or our friendship."

"I don't think you understand," Molly says, "I can handle any damage which you dish out."

"You might be able to," Zack replies with a sad smile, "but I'm not all that certain that I can."

Molly rises from the couch and takes the two glasses to her small sink.

"I want you to wait right here," Molly says as she disappears into the small dressing closet to the right kitchen area.

"I've to get up by 6," Zack replies.

"You wait right there," Molly says sternly.

Zack weighs the cost of not doing what Molly demands. In two minutes, Molly comes out of the closet in a sheer, short night gown. Zack can see that she has nothing underneath.

"I bought this especially for you," Molly says as she does a modeling pose and turns herself around in a pirouette.

"Molly," Zack says, "believe me when I tell you that you look stunning. If I were not the crazy person that I am, I would be seriously tempted to do something about it."

"I love the crazy person that you are," Molly says. "I bought this in the hope that will do something about it."

"I know and that's exactly why I can't do anything about it," Zack says as he rises from her couch.

Molly walks to Zack and presses herself tightly against him.

"Are you sure?" Molly says in whisper.

Zack grabs Molly by the shoulders and moves her backward a foot.

"Until I get myself sorted out," Zack says, "you know we can't start something which is going to complicate our lives even more."

"When are you going to have yourself sorted out?"

"By the end of June," Zack replies. "I swear."

"That's when that Hanover girl gets married isn't it?" Molly says heatedly.

Zack nods his head.

"Explain to me why it's her decision to make and not yours" Molly demands.

"Because that is how things work," Zack responds.

Molly shakes her head angrily.

"You're letting that bitch play you for the fool," Molly says hotly.

Zack draws Molly six inches nearer.

"I wish it wasn't that way," Zack explains. "You can't believe how much I wish that it wasn't that way, but that is the way that it is."

Molly backs away from Zack and goes to the ladder at the far end of the couch.

"You wait right here," Molly demands again.

In less than thirty seconds she has returned with a yellow silk sheet, two pillows in matching pillow cases and a light blue knitted blanket. She reaches under the couch and flattens it into a standard sized bed. Zack watches in uncertainty as Molly fits the sheet around the flattened couch, sets the blanket atop it and plops the two pillows on window side.

"Take off your shoes," Molly instructs.

Zack hesitates for a full 30 seconds before pulling off his tan deck shoes and setting them below the television mounted on the wall of the kitchen cabinet.

"Lay down," Molly demands as she pushes Zack gently toward the couch-bed.

Zack does as instructed as Molly switches off the lights.

"We aren't going to do anything," Molly says as she climbs over Zack, "unless you have a sudden change of heart."

Molly presses herself against Zack.

"I want you to hold me," Molly says, "I want you to keep holding me until at least 6AM." Molly pauses, then says in trembling whisper, "Then you can either keep holding me or you can go off to your workout without saying a word."

Night Out

Thursday, March 13, 7:22PM. Zack is seated in the passenger's seat of Abe's Volvo station wagon. Beth is driving. The car is in the hold of the ferry about 5 minutes from the dock at Halifax. The pair are on their way to take in one of Alfie's performances at 'Jewel's'.

"You think we are okay on time?" Beth asks.

"We'll be fine," Zack replies. "Alfie told me as long as we are at the bar by 8:15, he'll make sure we are seated before his first performance.

This past Monday, Zack had called Alfie to see how he was doing. The kid sounded fine. He'd invited Zack to come out and see him perform. When Zack had mentioned it to Beth, she'd ask if she could come along.

When Zack had shown up to pick up Beth, she suggested that they take Abe's car to avoid the distraction that driving Zack's battered VW was likely to cause. It had gotten so bad that people were now coming up to the car and asking for autographs when Zack was at a stop sign or traffic light.

"I think that we finally have the Paris trip worked out," Beth says. "You'll likely need to kick in around $4,000."

"I'm good with that," Zack replies.

"Have you been doing much related to Saanvi's wedding?" Beth asks.

"Other than listening to my mom and Saanvi argue and being fitted for a gold brocade sherwani," Zack replies, "not really."

"What are your mom and sister arguing about?" Beth asks.

"Saanvi wants to keep the wedding as simple as possible," Zack replies. "I think mom still wants something straight out of Bollywood."

"Who is winning?" Beth asks as the ferry announces that will be arriving at the Halifax pier in a few minutes.

"I don't think that we are going to know until the wedding takes place," Zack replies.

"How is your planning coming for the concert in Hanover?" Beth asks.

"Good as far as I can tell," Zack replies. "Molly and Dave are going over to Hanover tomorrow to set things up. Hopefully we won't have rain."

"How many people will be attending?" Beth asks.

"The Hanover facility people are saying around 5,000."

"Have you ever performed in front of that large of a crowd?" Beth queries.

"Nope," Zack replies. "Molly has been informed that crowd may be even larger as there is a huge demand to attend from the surrounding military bases."

"Doesn't that make you happy?" Beth asks.

"I'm not sure," Zack says tentatively. "I'm really looking forward to performing for everyone at the Hanover Medical Facility. If the audience turns out to be mainly yoyos and Ruperts, I am going to be bummed out."

"What are yoyos and Ruperts?" Beth asks with a crooked grin.

"Something my oppos call members of the officer class," Zack replies with an impish grin.

"What's an oppo?"

"How regular soldiers refer to each other," Zack answers as the ferry begins slowing to pull beside the pier.

"It's almost as if you guys come for a different universe," Beth remarks.

They are silent until the ferry is brought to a stop and the exit gate begins to open. Beth starts up the Volvo. There are only twelve cars in the hold on this Thursday evening. Once the gate is lowered, Beth steers the Volvo out of the ship's hold and turns left at the traffic light just past the ferry entrance. She drives for a mile and half until they pass in front of 'Jewel's'. Zack notices a group of about twenty protesters across the street from the bar.

"Are those Ainsley's people?" Zack asks.

"May very well be," Beth says. "I've been told there are still about 80 of them living in the compound which New Jericho is building on the west end and at least another 100 or so here on the Mainland."

"Ainsley being jailed hasn't killed off the church?" Zack responds somewhat incredulously.

"It's cut the New Jericho members in half," Beth replies. "The problem is that the half which are left are hard core Ainsley followers. Those remaining followers believe that shortly, Ainsley is going to be released from jail and all the charges brought against him will be dropped. When that happens, God's war will begin. Those followers have been laying low for the time being but the closer we get to Ainsley going to trial, the likelier it becomes they will cause trouble."

Zack shakes his head. Beth goes another two blocks before pulling into a parking garage. They exit the Volvo and the parking garage and walk across the street to avoid being close to the protestors.

A burly security guard is at the front of Jewel's. He motions them through to the entry kiosk. Zack pays both $20 cover charges for them to enter.

"Sweetie," the woman dressed as Cher, who is managing the kiosk says, "aren't you that Zack Tillerman fellow. If you're not, you're a better impersonator than I am."

"Guilty as charged," Zack says sheepishly.

"You two wait right here," the impersonator instructs. She returns in 30 seconds with Alfie dressed in a slightly updated version of the Marlene Dietrich which Zack had seen him in at Wannasea Village. Alfie walks to Beth and hugs her. He holds out his hand to Zack.

"You can hug me too, you know," Zack with a mock frown.

Alfie smiles and gives Zack a firm hug. Holding on to him just a few seconds longer than is appropriate.

"Will that do, big boy?" Alfie says batting her false eyelashes and using her Marlene Dietrich voice.

Zack nods his head sheepishly as Alfie leads them to a booth in the second row back from the stage. 'Jewel's' is a large venue. Zack estimates the place has the potential to hold more than 'the Shell'. At the moment, it is approximately 90% full.

"I'm really glad you guys came," Alfie says as he seats them in the booth and slides in beside Beth. "I can only sit with you for a minute or so. A girl's gotta' work, you know."

"How's it been going?" Beth asks.

"Really good," Alfie replies with a smile. "I think you'll see that my act is getting better. I'm also making much more than I planned. I've brought in over $1,000 in tips in my first week and this week looks like it will be even better. Doesn't look like I'm going to have to find a day job."

"What will you do with you time during the day?" Beth asks.

"Buy clothes," Alfie replies, "learn new songs, get my routines down pat."

"How long have those people been protesting out there?" Zack asks.

"Since long before I came here," Alfie replies. "The owner got a court order which keeps them across the street. We basically just ignore them."

'No troubles when you get off work?" Zack queries.

"We go out the back," Alfie replies, "Listen I got to get back to earning. What do you guys want to drink?"

"Ginger ale for me," Beth says.

"Orange juice," Zack requests.

Alfie scoots off to get the drinks.

Beth surveys the crowd. After a few minutes, she says to Zack in a lowered voice, "I have never felt so unglamorous in my entire life."

Zack hesitates for a few seconds before replying, "You are always glamorous, Beth."

"You are a real sweetheart for saying that," Beth says patting Zack on his hand, "but you are also a damned liar."

Two autograph seekers dressed in western outfits walk up to the booth.

"May we have your autograph" the one dressed like Jessie from Toy Story 2 asks as she slides a pen and two slips from a notepad toward Zack.

Zack complies with the request.

Four more people come to the table requesting autographs before Alfie delivers the drinks. Alfie sets them down, before scooting off toward the side of the stage.

"I'm on in a minute," Alfie explains. "You've seen this one. It's Marlene Dietrich but I've added a few new wrinkles."

Beth sips her drink as Zack signs two more autographs before Alfie is announced through the loud-speaker system.

"We are pleased to present the Blue Angel," comes through the audio system.

Unlit cigarette in hand, dressed in a tight-fitting tuxedo with bowtie, Alfie undulates to the middle of the stage. Alfie sings "Lilli Marlene" in German first. Halfway through the song, Alfie pulls away the tuxedo suit pants to reveal a high cut, skintight body suit and fishnet stockings. Alfie begins singing in English. Alfie vamps her legs and gestures with the cigarette as she sings. She ends the song by turning away from the crowd and wrapping her arms around her back as if she is being held in a tight embrace. As the crowd cheers and claps, Alfie breaks into "Falling in Love Again". Just as he had in Wannasea Village, Alfie has the house roaring as he does the line, "I was made that way". The crowd hoots and hollers as Alfie leaves the stage.

Zack has noticed during the performance that Alfie seems to be lip-syncing the songs but the voice being heard is Alfie's.

"That was quite something," Beth says to Zack. "That kid has a ton of talent."

Alfie comes back into the main audience area dressed exactly as she left the stage and immediately goes to work filling drink orders. For the next 20 minutes, she can be seen rapidly moving back and forth between tables and the bar. During this time, Zack signed five more autographs.

"I knew you are getting famous," Beth says to Zack as he signs the latest autograph request. "I didn't realize it has come this far."

"Don't get me wrong," Zack whispers to Beth. "I really like doing things for my fans but it's almost getting to the point where I don't have a life of my own anymore. I can't even go to the drug store to pick up my prescriptions. I have Molly do it for me."

Alfie comes to their table and sits down.

"Sorry," Alfie says, "I've learned that if I want tips, I need to hustle out here after my act and start pushing drinks. My problem is figuring out who will give me the biggest tips."

'You really were good," Beth says to Alfie. "I had no idea how talented you are."

"Thanks," Alfie says, "that means a lot to me."

"I notice that you are no longer singing the songs as you are performing," Zack says to Alfie.

"I've learned the act is much more about the performance and attitude," Alfie replies. "Most of the girls here don't sing. They are just extremely good at lip-syncing. Since I like to sing and my imitations are pretty good, they have let me record my own songs. In my case, it's helped out as it allows me to focus on physical movements. For the moment, I've got to work on how to interact with the crowd."

"You ought to figure out how to make better use of that voice," Zack suggests.

"I'll work on it once I've gotten my performance routines down," Alfie replies. "If you can think of any way to help me, I'm open to suggestions."

Four more people come to the table requesting autographs as Beth shares gossip from back at 'the Place' with Alfie.

"Got to get back to work," Alfie says rising from the booth. "I'll be back in about forty-five minutes. I want to make sure that you are here to watch that one. It's much different than what I did over in Wannasea."

Zack signs fourteen more autographs and they listen to three performers do various routines. The first lip-syncs to Britney Spears. The performer jokes with the crowd, something Alfie had not done. That set ended with "Baby One More Time". The second performer is even more adept at wisecracking with the audience. She lip-syncs to Donna Summer. Bringing three members of the audience up on stage to dance with her to "She Works Hard for the Money". The next performer is the person who had taken their entrance fee. Like Alfie, this performer does her own singing. She banters with the audience between songs. She ends her set by coming out into the audience and sitting down in Beth and Zack's booth. She wriggles up next to Zack and sings "Just like Jesse James" to him. She kisses Zack's cheek as the song ends.

"This is the most fun that I had since forever," Beth tells Zack with a laugh after the applause has stopped.

Before Alfie comes out on stage, a dressing screen is rolled out on the stage. After thirty seconds, Alfie appears from behind it dressed in auburn colored shoulder length wig, cut-off shorts, a black tank top, frilled jacket, and cowboy boots. Alfie does Miley Cyrus' "Party in the USA". When the song is over, Alfie disappears behind the screen. The singing during the performance was pure Alfie. Not quite the same as Miley Cyrus but not that far off either.

Alfie reappears after 30 seconds in a short platinum blonde wig, skimpy white halter top and sheer white yoga tights. She breaks into Mylie Cyrus' "We Won't Stop". Alfie manages to take twerking to a new level. By the time the song is done, Alfie has many in the audience twerking in the aisles and singing, "we won't stop".

When Alfie disappears behind the screen, a chain with a large ball of some sort drops out of the rafters onto the center of the stage. Alfie reappears in seconds in one on the skimpiest white two pieces which have ever been produced and a pair of reddish-brown Dr. Martens Delany boots. As the song starts, the dressing screen moves backwards. Two stanzas into the song Alfie climbs atop the ball, grabs on to the chain and swings herself out over the crowd, provocatively moving her body to the motion of the chain. On the last stanza of the song as the ball swings toward the rear of the stage, it disappears into the darkness along with Alfie. The crowd remains motionless for a full ten seconds then breaks into applause.

"What do you think?" Beth asks Zack.

"I think that Alfie has moved way beyond where any advice which I can give is going to do anything for her career."

The concert

Sunday, March 16, 4:58PM. Zack is in the curtained wings of the stage which has been set up on the parade grounds at the Hanover military base. The NorthEnders are on stage, set up and ready to play. Zack is fidgeting nervously. He has not been this anxious since his first performance at 'The Place'.

Molly is standing beside him with her cell phone in her right hand. Earlier this morning, she, Zack, and Emily had come to Hanover in Zack's battered VW, which is now very visibly parked at the side of the stage. The military's director of the performance had specifically requested that Zack bring his Volkswagen along, thanks in large part to the pictures of the battered vehicle in the print media over the past month. The Bug has become almost as in demand as Zack. They had rented a large van which had brought over Randy, the instruments, and the band along with Josh. Randy and Josh are serving as roadies. Josh is doing double duty as the van driver. Dave had come over on Friday with his shop's van to bring a limited amount of audio equipment which had then been merged with equipment they had rented in Hanover.

"Now with no further ado," a trim, quite striking thirty-something female major announces through the microphone on the stage, "here is one of our own, Zack Tillerman."

Zack moves toward the microphone waving out to the crowd. He was moving much faster than Molly had told him that he should. At the moment, Zack's need is to get to the point of actually playing the first song.

"Hello everyone," Zack says as he reaches the microphone. "You cannot believe how happy I am to see all of you out here on this beautiful Sunday."

The crowd roars back at him.

"Although you may have heard the songs on our website," Zack continues, forgetting to put ZackTillerman.com in front of the word website, "this will be the first time that we are performing 'Iraqi Blues' anywhere. I wanted to call this album 'The Big Suck Blues". I think quite a few of you here today may understand why I wanted to do that. My partners thought otherwise. In any case, these songs belong to people like you."

Zack pauses for a second as the crowd cheers.

"After we play through the songs on our new album," Zack says, "we will take a 15-minute break. Write down any of songs of ours which you would like us to perform. At the break, pass your choices on to my two beautiful assistants, Molly, and Emily. We will then do our best to play them for you after the break."

Zack points to the pair, who are now standing at each end of the stage.

Zack nods to the band, who break into the first stanza of 'Dark Thoughts Come'. Zack joins them on his electric guitar as the crowd hoots and hollers. The song comes off better than Zack had expected. The past two weeks of rehearsal with the NorthEnders at the SouthTown studio seems to be paying off. They play the last stanza of the song twice to appease the crowd.

The moment the cheering begins to subside, they break into 'Don't Blame it on the Alcohol'. The crowd sings the line 'don't blame the alcohol' each time that it comes up. They follow this up with 'Flyin''. The crowd reaction to this song is less spirited than the first two songs.

They do 'Six Year Blues' next. Zack and the band really get into the song and the crowd responds to it.

As they break into 'Fallujah on my Mind', Zack nods his appreciation to the band. They play through the last stanza two additional times with the audience singing along. Zack is stunned that so many in the audience seem to know every word of the song.

Next, they play the first stanza of 'Victim of Circumstance' but Zack stumbles on the second stanza not remembering the line. He stops playing his guitar and motions to the band to stop. "Well," Zack announces through the microphone, "that turned into a real 'ball of chalk'. Guess I'd better get it right, before I find myself 'beasted'."

The crowd laughs reflexively before Zack begins the song again and gets through it correctly. By the second stanza, the crowd is singing the 'victim of circumstance' line along with Zack.

Next Zack and the band do 'This Side of Nowhere Blues'. Zack is not surprised when the crowd sings "no shits left to give" along with him.

Hard Slog comes next. Each 'hard slog' line is sung out loudly by the crowd.

"This next song," Zack says into the microphone, "is the first one which I wrote for 'Iraqi Blues'. It is about my two best mates when I was a Treadhead in Big Suck Land. They spent their lives constantly being shortchanged. An example is their having only received two bottles of Laphroaig for taking me off the hands of the L team in the 'Armoured Cavalry'. Anyway, this song is for Clint, Hi and all our other fallen comrades'."

They do 'Chadwick & Williams'. The audience turns quiet as Zack sings. When the band has stopped, Zack repeats the last line without singing it to complete silence.

"Chadwick and Williams are gone

like it or not, we still live on"

They go immediately into playing 'What we do to ourselves'. It is the third stanza before the crowd begins singing 'what we do to ourselves' along with Zack.

They break into 'Gunbarrel blues'. The crowd becomes raucous and belts out every line.

'Quicksand of Time' comes next. Although the audience sings some of the lines, the enthusiasm drops off.

They finish out the set with 'What more'. The crowd sings the refrain.

"That's it for the 'Iraqi Blues' set," Zack says. "We'll be back in fifteen minutes. Tell Molly and Emily what you would like to hear."

Zack is surprised to find that he is sweating as profusely as if he had been down at the beach doing his work out. He follows the band behind the curtains and walks down the steps with them to the little area behind the stage. There is a nice breeze blowing.

"I think it was a great set," Jerome says as he lights a cigarette.

"Would have been if I hadn't blown the start of 'Victim of Circumstance'," Zack replies somewhat sheepishly.

"I thought you did that on purpose," Jerome replies after a drag on his smoke. "The crowd loved it."

"The lady running the stage says we have to end by 7," Josh announces as he comes around the back of the stage to where Zack and band stand.

Zack glances at this watch, 6:11. There is likely only going to be time for five or six more songs.

Molly comes around the corner and walks up to Zack.

"The consensus is that they'd like you to replay the whole album again," Molly says with a smile.

Zack shakes his head, "We can only do another 35-minute set. The power-which-is says we have to be done by 7."

"Yeah," Molly replies. "The lady, who introduced you, said that they have not made arrangements to have the lights turned on, so we have to be done by dark. How do we deal with it?"

"Were you keeping track of how the audience responded to each song?" Zack asks Molly.

"I did," Molly replies. "I've got it right here in my tablet."

"I don't want to do 'Chadwick and Williams' again because all I think we can do is diminish what we did in the first set," Zack says. "I want to finish up with 'Dark Thoughts Come'. What song do you think had the worst response?"

'Flyin;," Molly replies as she glances at her laptop.

"What I'd like you to do is match the remaining ten songs in pairs," Zack says. "The first pair will be the best response against the one which you think had the worse response. The second will be the next best against next worst and so forth. We'll ask the crowd to decide which one they want us to play."

"Give me a couple minutes," Molly says as she goes around the corner and leans against the trunk of Zack's VW.

Zack follows her and sits on the driver's side bumper breathing in the cool air. Five minutes pass before Molly moves around to where Zack is and shows her the choices.

"Looks good," Zack says. "Now the only other thing that I'm going to need is for you to come on stage between each song and help decide what the audience wants to hear."

Molly gives Zack a wide-eyed look of fright.

"I don't like going on stages," Molly says nervously.

"Should I ask Emily if she will do it?" Zack asks.

Molly gives Zack the stink eye.

"I'll do it," Molly says stubbornly, "but I am certainly not going to like it."

Jerome and Lamont walk past them on their way back up to the stage. Zack and Molly fall in line behind them.

Zack messes around with the tuning of his guitar for a few minutes until the crowd gets settled.

"Like many of you," Zack says into the microphone, "I went from a Crow to a Mucker to a Full Screw. Like some of you, I became a CaseVac after I got my ass shot off just outside of Hit."

The crowd roars.

"Despite all of that," Zack says, "the powers-which-be have dictated that we must have ENDEX of this get together no later than nineteen hundred hours. That only leaves time for 6 more songs. I'm going to pull rank and pick the final song. For the other five, I've asked the beautiful and very talented Molly to help you choose between two songs which you have indicated you would like to hear."

Zack backs away from the microphone and gestures for Molly.

"The first song choice is between 'Six Year Blues' and 'What More'," Molly instructs. "The loudness of your response will determine which song it is."

"How do you feel about 'What More'?"

There is loud hooting and hollering.

"Six Year Blues?"

The response is even louder.

"'What More' it is then," Molly instructs as she backs away from the microphone.

Zack decides that Molly is who doesn't want to hear 'Six Year Blues'.

The band does 'What More' hard and driving. The crowd loudly sings,

>"die or live
>what more
>can we give" .

Zack backs away from the microphone.

"The next choice is between 'Fallujah on my Mind' or 'Victim of Circumstance'," Molly announces.

"Fallujah on my Mind" is the clear winner.

The audience shouts out the lines which include "Fallujah on my mind".

"Our next choice is between 'GunBarrel Blues' and

'Quicksand of Time'," Molly decrees.

'GunBarrel Blues' is the popular choice.

The crowd sings most of the song with Zack.

"Next, we choose between 'Hard Slog' and 'What we do to ourselves'.

'Hard Slog' wins by volume.

The audience forces the last stanza to be done two extra times.

'Finally," Molly announces as twilight comes, "and this will be a hard one, 'Don't Blame the Alcohol' or 'This Side of Nowhere'."

By the slimmest of margins 'Don't Blame the Alcohol is judged the victor.

The crowd is loud and strong on this song. Zack checks his watch as the band reaches the next to the last stanza. There is time to repeat the refrain only twice.

"Blame me for this pick," Zack says as he leads the band into 'Dark Thoughts Come'.

They play the song until **darkness comes**.

"Thank you everyone," Zack says into the darkness. "May happiness fill all your coming days."

The crowd roars as Zack carries his guitar into the wings. Molly gives him a hug.

"I take it that you aren't a fan of 'Six Year Blues', " Zacks says with an impish smile.

"Never will be," Molly says grinning right back at him.

Zack walks over to Randy and Josh.

"Would it be okay with you guys if Randy rides back to the island with Dave," Zack asks. "I think he's going to need a little help getting what belongs to him into the van and making sure the rental company gets the rest of the equipment.

"Sure," Randy replies, "I'm good with it as long as Dave plans to stop for dinner."

"I can guarantee you," Zack says with a smile, "Dave will be stopping for dinner."

The brothers move off to help the NorthEnders load their equipment into the rental van.

As Zack and Molly stand to the side, Dr. Schiller and the major, who had introduced Zack, come through the entrance and walk toward them.

"Hi Doc," Zack says, "you remember Molly?"

"Indeed, I do," Dr. Schiller replies as he shakes Molly's outstretched hand. "That was a terrific concert. It did the people out there a world of good, Ralph. I hope you know how appreciative we are."

"It did me a lot of good too," Zack responds.

"This is Major Wallace," Dr. Schiller says gesturing toward the striking woman beside him, who is in full-dress uniform."

"Heather," the major says holding out her hand. "That was really a remarkable performance. I can't thank you enough."

"Thank you for having us," Zack says somewhat sheepishly.

"Being a former Mucker," the pert major says, "I guess you know what comes next?"

Zack looks at her somewhat quizzically.

"We are going to ask you to do more," the major says with a smile.

"Ask away," Zack responds.

"First I would like to see if you would come over to the hospital with Dr. Schiller and I and say hello to some of the patients over there, who were unable to make your concert?" the major requests.

"I'd love to," Zack replies.

"Great," the major says before continuing. "Secondly, we are wondering if you might have any interest in doing another concert in late May or early June at the Joint Strike Force base in Coventry?"

"I'm certainly willing to do that," Zack says. "Just get with Molly to establish the date."

"Wonderful," the major replies. "Now, and I must warn you that I'm being entirely too presumptuous here, would you consider going on a three-week entertainment tour in early December to bases in the Middle and Far East?"

The third request catches Zack completely off-guard.

"It's something I will definitely consider," Zack replies "but I'll have to see if I can adjust my schedule. Off-the-top of my head, the other big problem which we may have would be my band. All three of the guys are college kids. One graduates this May but the other two will still be in school in December. I don't see how they would be able to do it."

"If it will be of any help," Major Wallace replies, "I'm certain that we could provide you with accompaniment. As you yourself are a living example, we have some very talented people in the military. As long as you can decide if you are going by May 31st, I will do everything in my power to arrange it."

Tweed Conner

Wednesday, March 26, 1:24PM. Abe, Molly, and Zack are having lunch at the table closest to the kitchen door at 'Sam & Sallie's'. If a month or so ago Zack had thought that he was feeling the full impact of fame, he has now come to realize that he had been badly mistaken. Since the trio had set down to eat a little over an hour ago, Zack had been inundated with autograph seekers. The lunch, which Molly had arranged so they might discuss Abe's music catalog which remains in the hands of his agent, had been little more than non-stop interruptions. Zack didn't mind signing the autograph requests, but he was increasingly becoming resentful that some of those making autograph requests also wanted to hold a lengthy conversation. It was suddenly as if his entire fan-base knew his life story.

The restaurant is packed. There is a twenty-person line waiting outside to gain entrance. The casino opened almost 2 weeks ago. Now, almost every day, the restaurant is full, opening to closing.

Sallie comes out of the kitchen and sits down on the empty chair at their table.

"As soon as you are ready to go," Sallie tells them, "I'll lead you out the back way."

Molly and Abe have finished their lunch. Zack, who has only been able to grab a few bites, rises from his chair.

"Let's go," Zack says as he sees a young couple heading his way from across the crowded restaurant.

As they wait to follow Sallie into the kitchen, Zack pulls two-hundred-dollar bills from his wallet and slides them under his napkin.

"I think my days of eating out are about finished," Zack says as they move into the bustling kitchen.

"Next time, I'll set you guys up a table in the back where we are going to service the Event Center," Sallie tells them.

After they say hello to Sam, Sallie guides them out the side door beside the service window to the foyer of the Event Center. They walk through the empty foyer and to the main entrance doors. Sallie enters a code into the security box to the side of the door.

"Push the bar on any of the doors and you should be able to get out," Sallie says.

"Thanks a million, Sallie," Zack calls back as they walk into a slight drizzle.

"How long has it been like this?" Abe asks Zack in reference to the autograph requests.

"Until about a month ago," Zack replies, "it was tolerable. Now I can't seem to go anywhere without getting mobbed. It's even starting to become a real hassle getting in and out of my appearances at 'The Place',"

"He needs to think about getting a security detail," Molly suggests.

"Either that or moving to a much less populated island," Zack says.

They walk across the parking lot and through the open entrance to the Historical Society.

"Let's go sit in the main hall," Abe suggests.

The trio turns to the right walking down the hallway past the office and through the open doors of the main hallway. There is a person on the right-hand side of the seating area setting up camera equipment.

"We've started turning my talks into a podcast," Abe explains. "I'm not all that happy with video we are getting though."

"You should come over to SouthTown and talk with Dave," Zack suggests.

"That's probably a good idea," Abe says as he leads them to chairs in the front row.

When Zack and Molly are seated, Abe swings the empty chair next to them around so that it faces them and sits down.

"What's the deal with Reuven Cross?" Abe asks.

Reuven Cross is the principle in the group which had served as Abe's agent. On the first of the month, Abe's interest in his music catalogue was transferred to Zack at Abe's request.

"We think he wants to dump handling your music catalogue," Molly says.

"Considering the last quarterly check which I got from them was just a hair over $900," Abe says, "I'm not all that surprised. Alf certainly did an excellent job of finally killing off the 'Reggie Revival'".

The revelation that Reggie Reginald served as a drug mule for most the past 30 years, along with having a long history of impregnating young women has drained most demand for his songs.

"Cross offered to sell us his interest in the songs for $75,000," Zack says.

"Of course, he did," Abe says. "That's quick money for them and they don't have to bother to continue to flog a dead horse."

"He also is pushing us to sign on with them as our agents," Zack says.

"Him and about five hundred other talent agencies," Molly adds.

"You aren't considering it, are you?" Abe queries.

"I'm certainly not," Molly says firmly.

"They are one of the few agencies which have indicated that they are willing to honor my restriction on not doing any performance off this island," Zack adds.

"You have moved way past my level of knowledge on what's required to help your career," Abe says, "but I still think that I know enough to tell you that the Cross Agency is not going to be your answer. From what I hear, you are selling songs in places Cross has no presence and no experience."

"Honestly Abe," Zack says, "I'm not all that certain that I'm concerned about how many recordings that we sell. I'd be perfectly fine going back to how things were last year."

Abe smiles, "There's no going back. You can only go forward. In my more than 50 years in that business, the one thing that I can tell you from experience is that you cannot force success back into the bottle after it has escaped or has dissipated."

"The problem is that we are going to have to do something very soon," Molly says. "Zack seems to think we can just take an extended vacation and it will all go away."

"You better take stock of what you have first before you start wishing it away," Abe says. "Can you give me an idea of where ZackTillerman LLC stands right now?"

"We are closing in on the sale of two million copies of 'Iraqi Blues'," Molly replies.

Abe whistles his surprise.

"And everyone, their brother and their sister seem to want to grab a piece of it," Zack adds.

"Let me ask you something Zack," Abe inquires, "This desire not to perform off the island doesn't have anything to do with being worried about how the 'The Place' would be impacted if you no longer perform there, does it?"

"I won't say that isn't something which I haven't thought about," Zack responds, "but it's only a small consideration. The reality is that I don't really feel comfortable performing anywhere off the island."

"Wasn't that concert you had last week at Hanover a big success?" Abe asks. "Didn't you enjoy that?"

"I felt okay doing it because it was for my mates," Zack replies, "but I was mighty glad to get back out here and have a Wednesday night doing folk and sea songs."

Abe weighs Zack's response for a few moments.

"When I got into ZackTillerman ," Abe begins, "my intention always was to back out as soon as I thought you had things going in the right direction. Once I discovered my grandmother's journals, I knew that time was going to come sooner than I had imagined. Working with ZackTillerman was sort of like working with a baby until it learns to walk and becomes a toddler. In your case, you didn't just learn to walk, you learned to run. You are now running faster than I can keep up. What you should consider doing is seeing if you can find someone or some agency which is able to not only able to run with you but wants to go in the same direction you want to go."

"I'm not sure the direction which each of us want to go is the same," Molly interjects.

Abe gives them an odd smile before continuing, "Then before you do anything else, shouldn't the two of you figure out which direction you want to go and what part, if any, you are willing to give up keeping ZackTillerman going?"

"We've been trying," Zack says.

"Then you need to try harder," Abe says alternatively looking them both in the eye alternatively.

After a full minute of silence, Abe says, "Are you sticking around for my talk?"

"That's the main reason why we came," Molly says.

"I kind of like the peace and quiet here," Zack says, "I may become a regular."

"Just don't tell anyone that you are coming," Abe suggests. "I've got to get up on the stage and set up. The next time you guys want to come out and do lunch before the talk, let me know."

"Count me in for next Wednesday,' Zack says.

"Okay," Abe says rising and putting the chair back in place. "Hope you like my talk."

"Thanks Abe," Zack says to Abe as walks on to the stage.

Abe goes to a table behind the podium and picks up his briefcase. He opens it and pulls out a set of 3 papers which are copies of pages 5-9 of the first journal. He sits studying them for a few minutes, writing notes in the margins.

By 2PM, twenty-two other people had come into the Main Hall. They are spread out throughout the seating area which can hold 120.

Abe, notes in hand, rises and ambles to the podium.

"Good afternoon, everyone," Abe says into the microphone. "Welcome to another Wednesday session on Alice Bailey's Wannasea journals. Today we are going to discuss an entry from page 5 of the first journal. If you wish to follow along, there is a copy of all the journals which may be downloaded from the Wannasea Historical Society website."

Abe pauses for a moment to refer to his notes, before continuing, "Since I first spied this entry in the journal it has puzzled me. I had never heard of Tweed Conner and the only reference to the tale told within the verse comes from other historical areas. As I've looked into it, I discovered that there have been a long line of Connors in Wannasea Village, which stretches back to the early 1700s. Tom Connor, the current Headmaster of the Wannasea Elementary school just beyond the Constabulary, is one of those Connors. I only wish that I could tell you what happened to this Tweed fellow after he allegedly scared off the French."

Abe pauses again.

"In any event, this is the journal entry to which I am now referring,

Tweed Connor

> forty-two winters besiege tosspot Connor,
> he who dost sweep soiled tavern floor,
> battered and bruised, so full of need
> he that be a tatter'd Tweed, manners to abhor
> all know where Connor's true talent lies,
> his treasure hunt, ye pursuit of unsober days,
> breath full of stale ale, dark deep-sunken eyes,

Tweed lives a life which none should praise.
midst the dark of Mainland's blackest death
vile Frogs coursed forward to loot and pillage

to smote and smite, cut short our breath
to burn to the ground dear Wannasea village
rum-addled mind did service to avoid thee plight
Tweed spied **de Grasse ships** at day's first light,

bleary were his eyes when Tweed Conner saw
banners of the Sun King bounce o'er the waves
dabs chimney soot about cheeks and jowls,
unearthly apparition risen from the grave
toward yon incoming French, Tweed Connor ran
screamin' out with voice as from the depraved,
"Save me soul, afore 'Black Death' kills Connor klan"
gold-trimmed empty hats served by scurvy knaves
reconsidered then hastened to amend vile plan
de Grasse, wild-eyed French looters and vengeful leaders
curtailed their mission and fast changed course
raised their sails and hastened their sailors
no need for Tweed his sickness to be endorsed
Old Tweed Connor caused thee Frenchmen to flee,
Delivering to safety thy isle of Wannasea

rum-addled mind did service to avoid thee plight
Tweed spied French boats at day's first light,
Old Tweed Connor caused thee Frenchmen to flee,
Delivering to safety thy isle of Wannasea."

Losing Control

Thursday, April 3, 11:52AM. Zack is riding the Vespa 946 which he purchased on Monday morning around the traffic circle to head up Mountain Way toward 'The Place'. He has a noon meeting with Beth and Molly at Beth's house. The cause for the meeting is last night's performance at 'The Place' having turned into something of a fiasco due to people forcing their way into the dining area to watch Zack play despite having no entry tickets. Crowd control is becoming an increasing problem not only for Zack but for 'The Place' in general.

The purchase of the scooter had been driven by Zack's acknowledgement that his battered VW Bug has become a flashing advertisement that "Zack Tillerman is here". Wherever the Bug is parked, almost immediately people will begin showing up. In the past week, Zack has had two warnings from his holiday trailer park management over the number of people arriving at his trailer. Moving the Bug down to the SouthTown recording studio has somewhat diminished the traffic. On the plus side, the move of the Bug has had a positive impact on Dave's audio business.

Zack wheels the scooter left into the driveway to 'The Place' then swings left again to go up the driveway toward the house. Zack parks the scooter by the side of the bathroom which is attached to the studio. Six comes scampering up to Zack, expecting a head scratch. Beth and Molly are seated at the rear patio table in front of plates of sandwiches and pitchers of tea and lemonade. Seeing that there is food on the table brings a smile to Zack's face as finding anywhere to complete a meal in peace is something else which is becoming increasingly difficult to arrange.

"Nice scooter," Beth says to him as Zack walks to the table.

"He paid almost as much for that scooter as he would have if he bought a car," Molly interjects.

Zack pulls his helmet off and places it on the empty chair at the end of the table.

"The scooter gives me a little bit of anonymity," Zack says as he takes off his windbreaker and sits down beside Beth. "Anonymity is what I am striving for these days."

"He's got a point," Beth says to Molly. "Who expects to see a recording star riding around on a Vespa?" "The helmet and sweats also help," Molly adds.

"What kind of sandwich do you want?" Beth asks.

"Turkey, bacon and swiss, if you've got it," Zack replies.

"I do," Beth says. "I actually remembered what you like.' Beth hands Zack a plate with the sandwich he requested as Zack fills his glass with lemonade.

"Where are my babies?" Zack asks.

"Arlette has taken them for a walk," Beth says.

Zack hungrily bites into the sandwich and has it half gone by the time that Molly is finished saying, "We have got to take some kind of action to prevent having any more incidents like last evening."

"I have gotten two warnings from Island Public Safety about being over the occupancy limit during your Wednesday concerts," Beth says. "The Constabulary has been very lenient with us so far. I know that you really like playing inside 'the Place", but I'm afraid your Wednesday night sessions inside are going to have to come to an end."

"We can try doing them in 'The Shell' and see how that works out," Molly adds.

Zack frowns. One of the bigger joys in this current life is playing the Wednesday night gigs with his father inside the dining area of 'The Place'.

"You do realize that you've probably become too in-demand to be playing out here altogether?" Beth states.

Zack grimaces and hesitates a moment before saying, "I do, but I honestly don't want to play anywhere else."

"Molly tells me that you can barely go to your trailer now," Beth says, "that you are now usually either sleeping on her couch or over at your studio."

Zack nods his head.

"Zack," Beth says shaking her head, "that's madness."

"I've been hoping the demand will blow over soon," Zack says.

Beth gives Zack a searching look and says, "Certainly seems as if things are headed the other direction. Everyone working down at 'The Place' is being constantly badgered by people asking how they can get in touch with you."

"Are you thinking of sacking me because I've become too popular?" Zack says with a sad grin.

"Zack," Beth says place her hand upon his arm, "we would never in a million years "sack you". Beyond all this current madness, you have become part of us. You are as much a part of 'The Place' now as Abe or I, but we've got to take steps to reduce the crowd out here when you are playing."

'I'm okay with moving Wednesday's outside," Zack says. "I'll talk with Dave about adjusting the audio system to accommodate it."

"We are going to have to do more than that," Beth says as Zack finishes the rest of his sandwich.

Beth pulls another wrapped sandwich from the tray and puts it on Zack's plate without asking.

"Like what?" Zack asks as he unwraps the second sandwich.

"End the Friday sessions," Beth replies. "Raise the price of your Saturday performance to $50 and the price for Wednesdays to $35."

Currently the Wednesday session entry fee is $20. Zack's Friday and Saturday performances are $35.

"That's going to cut out a lot of people with limited funds from being able to see us," Zack says.

"You can do free concerts once in while down in the park by the east lake," Molly rejoins. "You could also do some concerts over on the MainLand in larger venues. You've already committed to the concert in Coventry on June15th. Major Wallace says that there will be at least 15,000 in attendance. It's going to be inside the football stadium. Why don't you think about trying a few performances in a much larger venue?"

Zack takes a long drink of lemonade before biting into his second sandwich.

"I guess we do not have much choice," Zack says. "It has been getting a little dangerous trying to get myself out of 'The Place' when the sessions are over."

Zack has taken to sneaking out the back door while his father and the rest of the band play a few more songs. Increasingly he is finding that tactic ineffective.

"It's not much better for you at 'The Shell'," Molly adds. "You usually have to wait backstage for an hour until you can get out without being mobbed."

"We are going to take some steps to help with that," Beth says. "We will be putting in a gated and fenced driveway which leads to the loading area for the stage. I'm also having fencing put around the patio area. People have gotten in the habit of hanging out there while you are playing. We are going to start charging $10 to sit at the patio tables from an hour before your sessions until they are finished. We are also going to have three additional security guards around when you perform. Two of those guards will assist in helping you get in and out."

Zack ponders what Beth has said while he finishes the second sandwich.

"I've been thinking about redoing all the folk and sea song recordings which we have on the website," Zack says. "I guess I can use the extra time which I'll have to do that. I would really like to make those recordings from the stage at 'The Place'. Is there any chance I can use 'The Place' on Monday or Tuesday nights when we are ready to record?"

"Don't see why not," Beth says.

Arlette comes around the corner pushing the twins in a Mockingbird double baby carriage. Her son Gabriel, who is now 16 months, is in day care. Arlette wheels the carriage over to where Zack, Molly and Beth are seated.

"Sit down and have some lunch," Beth says to Arlette. "We'll handle these two guys."

Zack rises from his chair and walks to the carriage as Arlette sits down beside Molly.

"I'm going to pick up the first one of you that smiles at me," Zack says to the Twins.

Both Twins eyes sparkle as Zack talks to them, but it is Julia, who smiles first as Zack begins making goofy faces at the two.

Zack unbuckles her and lifts her from the carriage.

"Don't tell your brother that you are my favorite," Zack whispers into Julia's ear as he takes her back to his seat.

Beth picks up Nathan and brings him back to her seat.

After exchanging finger tugs, silly sounds and goofy grins with Julia, Zack begins softly singing "Wannasea Pirates" to her.

When Zack has finished with the song, Beth says, "I forgot that there is one other thing we need to discuss."

Zack looks at Beth quizzically.

"I had lunch with Saanvi on Tuesday," Beth says, "and she asked if you and I will do 'We Didn't Start the Fire' at her reception."

"My mum said Saanvi didn't want me playing any music," Zack responds, somewhat surprised. "Your mom didn't want you playing music," Beth replies. "She also didn't want any alcohol or dancing. Saanvi has hired a DJ and bar service. All of which are going to show up at the wedding just as soon as the Buddhist monks are gone. She asked that we sing the song before the DJ gets started."

A Wedding

Sunday, April 13, 2:13PM. Saanvi and Ray Simmons are seated in chairs at the front of the stage at 'The Place'. Prisha and her husband have just set a loop of thread on Saanvi's head. Ray's seventy-eight-year-old grandmother is placing the loop from the other end of the thread atop Ray's head. An array of lit candles is arranged upon small tables surrounding the couple.

The three Buddhist monks in front of the stage are chanting, "Nam-myoho-renge-kyo ".

A little over 100 people are seated inside of the dining room area of 'The Place' for the wedding. The majority of the attendees are friends, working acquaintances or relatives of Saanvi. Ray's contingent is limited to his grandmother, three of his college mates and four Press colleagues.

The chanting stops. The monk in the middle says, "As the Venerable Dhammananda Maha Nayaka Thera has said, "if a man can find a suitable and understanding wife and a woman can find a suitable and understanding husband, both are fortunate indeed"."

The other two monks pull out a string of thread. They immerse one end of the thread into a bowl of water which sits in front of a statue of the Buddha on a table behind the couple. The monks recite two prayers in the Pali language. The monks then make a paste out of the water and the wax taken from the burning candles. Each monk applies the paste to the foreheads of Saanvi and Ray as a mark of blessing.

"As we have are taught," the monk standing at the front says to Ray and Saanvi, "A family is a place where minds meet one another. If these minds love one another, the home will be as beautiful as a flower garden. But if these minds get out of harmony with one another, it is like a storm that plays havoc with the garden."

The other two monks chant, "Om mani padme hum",

"As our Scriptures tell us," the monk standing at the front continues, "Do not deceive; do not despise each other anywhere. Do not be angry nor bear secret resentments, for as a mother will risk her life and watch over her child, so boundless be your love to all, so tender, kind, and mild. Cherish good will right and left, early and late, and without hindrance, without stint, be free of hate and envy while standing and walking and sitting down, whatever you have in mind, the rule of life that is always best is to be loving-kind."

The other two monks now chant, **"Om Vasudhare Svaha"**.

Saanvi and Ray pick up a small card from their laps. They recite the words of Lama Thubten Yeshe in unison, "Today, we promise to dedicate ourselves completely to each other, with body, speech, and mind. In this life, in every situation, in wealth or poverty, in health or sickness, in happiness or difficulty, we will work to help each other."

The monk behind the bride and groom dips a slim blue feathered stick into the bowl of water, walks behind Ray and shakes water on to Ray's head. He repeats the water blessing with Saanvi.

All three monks rapidly chant, "Om mani padme hum" 108 times.

Saanvi turns to Ray and says, "I, Saanvi take you Ray to be my husband, my partner in life and my one true love.

I will cherish our friendship and love you today, tomorrow, and forever.

> I will trust you and honor you.
> I will laugh with you and cry with you.
> Through the best and the worst,

> Through the difficult and the easy.
> Whatever may come I will always be there.
> As I have given you my hand to hold
> So, I give you my life to keep."

Ray then turns to Saanvi and says, "I, Ray, take you Saanvi to be my wife, my partner in life and my one true love.

I will cherish our friendship and love you today, tomorrow, and forever.

> I will trust you and honor you.
> I will laugh with you and cry with you.
> Through the best and the worst,
> Through the difficult and the easy.
> Whatever may come I will always be there.
> As I have given you my hand to hold
> So, I give you my life to keep."

Again, the three monks chant, "Om mani padme hum" 108 times rapidly.

Pritha and her husband rise and jointly read these words, "For any beings who practice honestly, at any time; that time is the lucky time, the good blessing, an auspicious fortune, a shining dawn, a good moment, a good act of worship. For those who have such excellent practice, their physical actions are a rightful religious offering, their words are a rightful religious offering, and their intentions are a rightful religious offering. May your wishes be so rightful: all beings who have such rightful actions will receive their rightful benefits."

Followed by the lead monk saying, "May all heavenly beings rejoice in the well-being that is the merit that we have accumulated for the sake of attaining prosperity and success."

Prisha and Hank then pass gift envelopes to each of the monks.

"Our wedding ceremony is now complete," Saanvi announces. "We are going to take a fifteen-minute break before we proceed to the cake cutting, singing, dancing and just generally having a good time."

Saanvi and Ray rise from the stage and move to the table where Prisha and Hank sit. Beth and Marie rise along with Molly and Sallie and go into the kitchen. They return with large orange-mango mousse cake inscribed with "Congratulations Saanvi and Ray". Molly and Sallie follow with a cart filled with glasses of champagne and mimosas.

Zack fidgets in his chair next to his father. Zack is dressed in a gold brocade sherwani, silver pajama pants and gold-colored slippers just as his father and Ray are. The silver turban with the green feathers atop his head had begun to cause him to start to sweat profusely. Zack rises from his chair and walks back to the restroom.

He carefully removes the turban and runs cold water over this face and hair. He dries himself with paper towels. Holding the turban under his arm, he exits the restroom and walks out the rear exit. Zack stands outside for a few minutes, holding the door open. He breathes in the cooler outside air before placing the turban back atop his head and returning to the dining room. He moves to the kitchen end of the bar as Ray and Saanvi cut the cake. Molly brings a piece over to Zack after the majority of the other wedding guests have been served.

"Did you see the DJ?" Molly asks. "He ought to be here by now."

"I'll go out front and take look," Zack says, "just as soon as I finish my cake."

Molly returns to helping to hand out drinks while Zack downs his slice of cake. He then proceeds across the dining room and out the front entrance. He hasn't gone more than two more steps before he has his photograph snap at least five times by three different photographers. Zack does his best to ignore them. After looking through the parking lot for anything which might refer to "DJ Island Vibes". Finally, Zack spots a white utility van which has just pulled into the parking lot. Zack signals to the driver.

When the van is beside him, he rolls down his window.

"Just pull your van up to the front entrance," Zacks instructs. "I'll help you unload."

The driver studies Zack for a few minutes before saying, "You are Zack Tillerman, aren't you?"

Zack frowns and replies, "I was the last time I checked."

He follows the van to the front entrance, then helps the driver carry his equipment into 'The Place'. Once 'DJ Island Vibes' has brought all his equipment in and gone back out and parked his van, Zack helps him plug into the audio system.

"You play in here, don't you?" the DJ says.

"Not anymore," Zack says. "I'm only playing outside these days. Did they tell you that we are going to be doing a song before you start."

"The lady, who called me mentioned it," the DJ says. "What's the song going to be?"

"'We Didn't Start the Fire," Zack replies.

"Want me to do something which kinds of melds into it?" the DJ suggests.

"That would be great," Zack replies.

"Mind if I ask you, who has enough money to hire you as their wedding singer?" the DJ asks.

"Wasn't hired," Zack replies. "It's my sister's wedding."

"Nobody is going to believe me when I tell them that Zack Tillerman helped me set up," the DJ says.

"Do you have your cell phone with you?" Zack asks.

"Sure," the DJ says pulling it out of his pocket.

Zack calls for Molly to come over.

"Do you mind taking a couple of pictures of us setting up?" Zack asks Molly.

Molly takes the DJ's camera and takes four shots of the pair finalizing the set up.

Zack then walks back over to the bar, picks up a mimosa and slowly begins to sip it until Beth comes up to him.

"I think they are ready for us," Beth tells him.

Zack walks with Beth on to the stage. He pulls his electric guitar out from behind the wall-end of the piano bench. Zack then moves the microphone and stands to the side of the piano before positioning the main microphone at the front of the stage. He spends a further few minutes working with Beth to adjust their tuning. After the DJ has moved off the stage, Zack checks to make certain everyone has settled into their tables before saying, "At a special request from my sister, of whom I am so very proud, Beth and I are going to play one of her favorite songs."

Zack notices that the DJ seems to have begun recording on his cell phone.

Zack and Beth break into 'We Didn't Start the Fire'. They had practiced the song at Beth's studio on Friday afternoon for two hours at Beth's insistence. The Twins had not seemed to have liked their mother doing the song but those gathered in the dining area certainly did. Zack and Beth perform the song twice before stopping.

The DJ has queued Bill Joel's "Only the Good Die Young" to follow it up. As that song goes into the second stanza Zack walks up behind 'DJ Island Vibes' and whispers to him, "I don't care which of your friends you show that recording which you just made, but if I find that recording anywhere on the internet, I'm going to sue your ass off."

Unexpected Guest

Friday, April 18, 10:12PM. Zack has just walked off the stage at 'The Shell'. About halfway through tonight's performance, it had begun to thunder. Rain then could be heard pattering steadily on the structure of 'The Shell's' roof. Some of the fans on the upper reaches of the seating area had gotten a little wet but they had all stuck around until Zack finished tonight's session with 'Dark Thoughts Come'.

"Only four more Fridays to go," Jerome from the NorthEnders says.

Beth had cut-off ticket sales for Zack's Friday performances after May 16th.

"It's going to be weird not playing here on Friday," Zack replies. "Have you guys gotten anything lined up yet?"

"The Caves are going to take us for Thursday and Friday's starting the end of May," Jerome replies. "You can always come out and play with us if you get bored."

"You'll have to learn to do some reggaeton though," Clarence throws in.

"I'm okay with that," Zack says.

Zack walks over to the first of four armchairs which sit at the far end of the backstage area. He pulls his tablet from the inside pocket of his jacket which is draped over the arm of the chair before sitting down. He goes to work on turning the Tweed Connor poem into a sea song.

After the NorthEnders have taken their instruments to their van, Jerome comes back into the backstage area and says to Zack, "You may want to make a run for it while you can.

There's nobody out here and the radio is saying there are harder rains coming in about an hour."

"Thanks," Zack says as he rises from the chair and begins putting on his windbreaker. After placing his tablet into the jacket's inside pocket, he picks up his guitar from the beside of the chair and takes it to its case against the back wall. He puts the instrument inside and sets it against the wall. Zack puts on his windbreaker, then dons his helmet before heading for the exit. Rain is falling but it seems to have let up from what had been an hour ago.

Zack makes sure the backstage exit is locked before scooting down the steps and around the corner to where his Vespa is parked under the awning covering the service area. Zack drives past the fencing which is in the process of being put up on the new driveway which leads behind the patio area. The parking lot for 'The Place' is almost empty. He maneuvers the scooter down Mountain Way to the roundabout where he takes the first turn off on to South Road. The rain is beginning to pick up and bites into Zack face a little. It takes him two minutes more than his normal twelve to reach his trailer. Zack brings his scooter up on the deck and wheels it to the shed at the rear of the patio area. He puts the scooter inside, takes off his helmet and places it on the scooter's seat before exiting the shed and locking its door. Zack semi-trots to his trailer's entrance. After unlocking the door and stepping inside, he pulls the tablet out of his windbreaker and sets it on the counter. Zack pulls off his windbreaker and carries it to the laundry area at the rear of the unit where he tosses the jacket into the dryer. He pulls his wallet and keys out of his jeans then takes them off and puts them inside the dryer as well. He switches the unit on and listens to the click-click sound of zippers tumbling against the aluminum drum.

Zack goes into his bedroom and pulls off his shirt and throws it in the laundry before putting on a pair of sweatpants and T-shirt with a picture of the face of a baby panda on it. Zack walks back to the kitchen and fixes himself a cup of tea before picking up his tablet and walking into the living room area. He switches on the FM radio of his stereo and tunes to the Swansea classical music station before sitting down on the couch. He can hear the rain begin to pick up from the tapping on the top of the metal roof of his trailer.

During his ride back to the trailer, a refrain kept running through Zack's mind. "The rain keeps on fallin'". The entire ride back Zack kept singing it to himself mixing in other lines. Zack pulls his acoustic guitar from beside the wall end of his couch, He spends the next forty minutes coming up with a new song:

rain keeps on fallin' *129 BPM in the key of C Major in 4/4 time*

> as rain keeps on fallin'
> can't stop myself recallin'
> you left me crestfallin'
> there's no use in stallin'

> skies have turned as gray
> as a heartache which won't go away
> a wound which doesn't mend
> all I can do is pretend
> that I no longer care
> that we are no longer a pair

> as the rain keeps on fallin'
> can't stop from recallin'
> you left me crestfallin'
> there's no use in stallin'

> road wet as my eyes
> when I tell myself old lies
> pretending there's no regret

        as if we'd never met
        leaves me feeling alone
        won't I ever get home

        left alone and cryin'
        there's no use denyin'
        closer to despair I keep drawin'
        as rain keeps on fallin'

        can't stop myself
from taking misery down from the shelf
        everything neither here nor there
        no longer sure I belong anywhere
if this emptiness doesn't leave me today
first strong breeze will blow me away

        these aren't real tears that I'm cryin'
        only myself to whom I'm lyin'
        as rain keeps on fallin'
        the same old regrets are callin'

        these aren't real tears that I'm cryin'
        only myself to whom I'm lyin' "
        too much regret comes in recallin'
        as rain keeps on fallin'

        too much regret comes in recallin'
        as rain keeps on fallin'
        rain won't stop fallin'

A loud knocking comes from his trailer's front door. Zack reflexively glances at his watch which reads 11:32. Zack sets his guitar down beside the front of the couch's armrest. Zack switches off the stereo on his way past.

'This had better be Molly,' Zack thinks as he rises from the couch and heads toward the front door. 'If this is a reporter or another wannabe agent, I'm not certain that I am going to be able to prevent myself from roughing them up.'

He opens the front door a crack to see who is there. To his utter amazement, Abby stands before him drenched to the bone. Zack pulls upon the door. Abby enters shaking water from the light windbreaker she is wearing over her white shorts and orange top.

Before Zack is able to say anything, Abby blurts out, "Can't lie to myself anymore, RJ. I can't keep pretending that you are gone from my life. I can no longer ignore that I can't stop myself from wanting to be with you."

"But you are engaged to be married?" Zack responds as he gently leads Abby into the trailer and closes the door.

"The engagement is off," Abby reveals. "Ending the engagement is something which I should have done months ago."

"Let's get you dried off a little before we get into that," Zack says as he closes the front door and walks to the common bathroom where he pulls out a beach towel. He returns with it and holds it out to Abby, who is shivering. Zack wraps the towel around her and rubs it against her shoulders as he guides her back to the laundry room. He stops the dryer before saying to Abby, "Take those things off and throw them into the dryer. I'll go find you something for you to put on."

Abby begins complying as Zack walks to his bedroom and pulls out another pair of sweatpants and a Calvin and Hobbes T-Shirt, he carries them back to the laundry room where Abby is standing in her underwear drying her hair with the towel. Zack sets the clothes atop the dryer as Abby hands him the towel.

"I had to see you," Abby says as she pulls on the sweatpants. "I couldn't go any longer without seeing you."

Zack puts his hand on Abby's arm in a reassuring manner. Abby leans into him and hugs him tightly.

"Did you break off your engagement because of me," Zack asks as Abby presses against him, "or did you break it off because it was the right thing to do?"

"Both," Abby says. "I simply cannot continue to go on the way things have been."

"When did this happen?" Zack asks.

"Tonight," Abby replies. "Alex came over to Coventry and we got into a fight over my listening to your songs. I decided that I've had enough of his trying to control everything that I do. I threw his ring back at him and told him that I'm through. The past three hours I've spent driving over here, hoping to be able to find you."

Zack begins to pull away from Abby, but Abby moves with him.

"You aren't going anywhere until you kiss me, RJ," Abby states firmly moving her lips close to his.

As they kiss, Zack knows that this is a different Abby from the Abby of seven years ago. A sleeker more determined version. Not quite as yielding as she once was. Yet, she fills him with the same old warmth and longing. Abby does her best to squeeze out the last atom of empty space which separates them. Zack now knows that though the threads which keep his heart tethered to Abby may be frayed, they have not as yet been broken. He loses track of how long he has been kissing Abby. It almost seems as if the past seven years have melted away and he's been kissing Abby for eternity. Abby moves her lips away from his and continues to hug Zack for a full two minutes before gradually moving back a little.

"You can't believe how long I have been wanting to do that," Abby says looking deep into Zack's eyes as if trying to enter his very soul.

Zack knows that the same thing applies to him, but fear keeps him from saying it.

"How about a cup of tea?" Zack asks Abby as she begins putting on the t-shirt.

"That would be wonderful," Abby says as she picks up her wet clothes and the towel and puts them into the dryer.

Zack switches the dryer back on before Abby takes his hand and walks with him into the kitchen. Zack hands Abby a boxed selection of Pukka Relax teas. She sifts through them as Zack refills the electric tea kettle and turns it on.

"Are you hungry?" Zack asks.

Abby turns to Zack and kisses him full-mouthed.

"I'm hungry for you," Abby says breathlessly. "I hadn't realized it until a few moments ago, but I've but I haven't stopped being hungry for you for the past seven years."

Abby kisses him for the better part of three minutes.

As Zack reaches into the cabinet to get a mug for Abby's tea, he pinches himself hard on his left arm. He wants to make certain that he has not fallen asleep on the couch and is dreaming.

"There are so many things we need to sort out," Abby says as she presses herself against Zack and takes the mug from his hand.

There are too many miles and too much tribulation for Zack to shed his skin and return to his seventeen-year-old head-over-heel-in-love with Abby self, but he knows that this is likely as close as he is ever again going to come to being able to do it again.

Abby completes making her tea before they go to the couch, where Abby curls herself up as close to Zack as is possible.

"I was really starting to worry that I wouldn't find you tonight," Abby tells Zack. "I tried calling you as the ferry pulled into the pier, but I got a message that your phone wasn't in service."

Zack doesn't tell Abby this is likely due to his having removed her from his contacts which now causes her to be blocked from being able to reach him via cell phone.

"I stopped at 'The Place" and didn't see your car. This was my last hope for tonight."

"It was a lucky coincidence," Zack replies. "This is only the second time this week that I've been able to come to the trailer to sleep."

"Why?" Abby says in a surprised tone.

"If people see that I'm here," Zack begins, "they'll bang on the door. Seven in the morning. Eleven at night. It doesn't matter. It's gotten so bad that I've parked my Bug down at the SouthTown studio and most nights I sleep there on the couch."

Zack decides not to tell Abby that he also sleeps at Molly's occasionally.

"Why don't you just get yourself another place?" Abby says. "Somewhere with security which will keep people from coming to your door when you don't want them to."

"I'm not really the kind of guy who lives in a secured complex," Zack says. "I spent too much time in Iraq living that way."

Abby looks at him quizzically as she takes a sip of her tea.

"You have some very strange ways, RJ," Abby says with a chagrined smile.

Abby picks up Zack's tablet and studies it.

"What' this?" Abby asks.

"It's a new song that I'm writing," Zack responds.

Abby reads the words again.

"Play it for me," Abby requests.

"I haven't even played it for myself yet," Zack replies.

Abby leans across Zack and kisses him deeply.

"Play it for me anyway," Abby responds.

Zack picks up his guitar from the end of the couch. He fiddles around with the tuning for a few minutes as he considers adjusting the melody. He finally plays it the first way that he'd written it.

"You wrote this yourself?" Abby asks.

Zack explains the lyrics which had been running through his mind as he drove the Vespa back to the trailer.

"You wrote this in like 30 minutes?" Abby asks.

"More or less," Zack replies.

"Why don't you try it in the key of A?"

Zack adjusts the tuning of his guitar and plays it through in the key of A Major.

"I like it that way better," Abby says.

"I think I do too," Zack replies.

Abby takes Zack left hand and entwines it in her two slightly smaller hands.

"It's a little dark though," Abby says. "How did you become so dark RJ?"

Before Zack can stop himself from saying it, he blurts out, "I've had seven years of practice."

Performances

Saturday, April 19, 7:21PM. Backstage at 'The Shell', Zack has just introduced Abby to the NorthEnders.

"How did you meet this guy?" Jerome asks Abby as the three band members stand circled around Zack and Abby.

Abby has her arm around Zack's waist and is pressed tightly against his side. Just as she had been most of the past day. "When we were fifteen," Abby begins, "RJ and I were in a string quartet at the Hanover Conservatory. The first time I met Zack was at our rehearsal. He was a little rougher around the edges then."

Zack and Abby had driven up to 'The Shell' in Abby's custom 2012 Mini-Cooper S five minutes previous. The car was cream colored with wine-red top and black rims with matching trim.

"RJ was the most serious musician I had ever met," Abby says. "I had an immediate crush on him. It took me almost a year to get the idea into RJ's head that I liked him. I swear I was almost ready to bop him over the head with my violin if he didn't start noticing me."

"Good to know, RJ's always been the serious type," Clarence says. "We thought he was just that way around us."

"All of the girls in our quartet had a crush on him," Abby says, "but RJ was too absorbed in his music to realize it."

That is not quite how Zack remembers it. The other two girls in their quartet had always been lukewarm toward him. Even before he had been kicked out of the Conservatory.

"What did RJ play in this quartet?" Jerome asks.

"The cello," Abby replies with bright smile. "He was very good at it."

Zack had forgotten how captivating Abby could be. It was one of the first things that he had recognized in Abby back in their Hanover days. It was also why Zack had a hard time imagining that she would ever have an interest in him.

"Do you guys play together anymore?" Jerome asks.

"We do when we have the chance," Abby says giving Zack a little hug.

Zack notices Molly walking in through the rear entrance. As his eyes meet Molly's, Zack sees her smile until the moment Molly recognizes who is standing next to him. The anger and frustration coming from Molly then seems to become almost palpable.

Zack thinks perhaps if he introduces Abby to Molly, her anger will subside but by the time Zack has turned to Abby to walk over for an introduction, Molly has bolted and gone out the backstage door.

"We better go finish getting set up," Jerome says. "It was great meeting you, Abby. Hope we see a lot more of you around here."

"You certainly will if I have anything to do about it," Abby says.

Zack kisses Abby on the cheek and pulls away from her to collect his guitars from their cases against the back wall. He carries both out to the stage and sets them beside the stool which sits behind the microphone. Shouts of "Zack, Zack" rise from the crowd as he turns and walks back into the backstage area. The band begins tuning up. The shouts of "Zack, Zack" become louder. The band slowly breaks into the first stanza of 'Don't blame it on the Alcohol'. Abby pulls Zack to her and kisses him with urgency. Zack can feel Abby's heart beating against his chest. She gently pushes him away from her and out toward the stage.

Zack can't stop himself from looking back at Abby. She has on a light green flared sleeve dress imprinted with roses and surrounding nosegay. Abby had put on the dress earlier in the day when they had gone out to her parents' villa. With Abby's parents currently being in Greece until the middle of next month, Abby had convinced Zack that they should move their base for the weekend to the Villa. Zack takes one last look at Abby, hoping to permanently imprint the image of her on his brain, before he turns and faces the crowd.

Zack lifts both his arms and waves to the crowd. As the volume of the shouts increases, Zack picks up his electric guitar. Before beginning to play, he pats his chest over his heart and blows a kiss out to the crowd. Zack cannot remember having ever done a first set with as much energy as he has tonight.

At the break, Zack walks to the wings and Abby hands him a clear plastic cup full of unsweet iced tea. Zack has no clue how Abby managed to get the tea. During his performance Zack had kept looking into the wing to make sure Abby was still there. She had not seemed to have moved even once. Zack takes a big sip of the tea, then takes hold of Abby's hand as they follow the NorthEnders out the back exit.

"You are so much better with the crowd than you used to be," Abby tells Zack as they walk around the band members, who are taking a smoke break.

There is a full moon. A wide variety of stars are shining in the clear night sky beyond the range of the haze from the lighting.

They walk to the newly installed fence and lean against it. Abby takes the cup of iced tea from Zack's hand and takes a sip of it.

"I keep thinking that I'm dreaming," Zack says to both Abby and the night sky.

Abby presses herself close against him, "But you're not. We are both here in flesh and blood and unless you chase me away, being with you is exactly where I'm planning on staying."

Zack wants time to come to a stop. He would be completely satisfied to lean against this chain-link fence with Abby for the rest of eternity.

"Penny for your thoughts," Abby says.

Her request brings back memories of those same words often being on Abby's lips from the days when they were seventeen. For the first time in seven years that memory doesn't bring instant regret.

"I'm hoping tonight never ends," Zack says squeezing Abby and turning to breathe in her scent.

"It doesn't have to," Abby says. "All we have to do is make sure that we do everything that we can to stay together."

"I'll sign up for that," Zack says.

Abby kisses his neck.

They stand gazing up at the night sky until noticing that the band has gone back inside. Hand-in-hand they head to the backstage area.

The next fifty minutes pass in a blur for Zack. He does most of the songs from his Iraqi Blues album. By the second song, Zack realizes that not only he, but his heart, is singing this evening.

When the second set is over and the crowd is done showing its appreciation, Zack disappears into the wings. Abby hands him a warm cup of chai.

"How are you coming up with these drinks?" Zack asks Abby. "There's this little red-headed guy, who helps the band with their equipment that asked me if he could get me anything,' Abby replies.

Zack thinks for a moment before realizing that Abby has spun her spell on Randy.

Zack stands in the wing sharing the chai with Abby until the crowd has gone. He walks back out to the stage and picks up his two guitars from the now dark stage. He closes and locks the door leading from the wing. Abby takes his acoustic guitar from his hand before Zack takes his electric guitar and places it in its case against the back wall. Taking first the acoustic guitar then Abby's hand, he walks with her out the stage door exit and to the Mini. Abby pops the small trunk, allowing Zack to place his guitar inside. After Zack closes the trunk lid, Abby tosses her keys to Zack.

"You drive," she says.

After climbing into the car and starting it, Zack turns the car around in the loading area and heads out the now fully gated driveway. At the gate, a burly security guard lets them out.

"Good concert," the guard calls to Zack as they merge into the parking lot of 'The Place'.

"Let's go for a walk down by the lakes," Abby suggests.

Zack maneuvers her convertible through the mostly empty parking lot to its rear east corner. Zack parks the vehicle in the last slot. He turns off the car. Hand in hand they walk through now slightly wet grass up the incline, across entrance to the driveway then across Mountain Way to the walking path around the lake.

"I used to come walking out here with my Aunt Sarah a lot when I was a little kid," Abby says. "I used to think that this was a magical place."

"It still is a magical place," Zack says. "I don't know of any place more magical."

"I used to think that there was a kind wizard, who lived here on this mountain," Abby tells Zack. "A wizard like Merlin, who protects the island and tries to make certain that nothing bad happens here."

Zack absorbs Abby's words for a few minutes as they walk slowly in the darkness toward the first lake.

"You know there actually is a kind of wizard, who lives here," Zack says to Abby with a big smile. "I'm going to call him up tomorrow and see if we can have breakfast with him."

Abby forces them to stop walking.

"You are joking, right?" Abby says with a laugh.

"Nope."

Off To See The Wizard

Monday, April 21, 9:28AM. Zack wheels Abby's Mini into the parking lot of Abe and Beth's house. Despite himself, Zack is beginning to enjoy driving Abby's Mini. Abby is holding a white cardboard box of pastries which they had purchased at Spillman's Bakery in the Village. Zack had had no earthly idea this particular bakery was in the Village. Abby seems to know a wide variety of things about this Island which had escaped Zack's attention.

Zack had called Abe yesterday to arrange to have breakfast with him. As Hugh and Helen were visiting, Abe asked if they could do it this morning.

They walk to the first patio table, where tea and coffee service has been set up. Abby places the box of pastries on the table.

"Let go see my babies," Zack says to Abby. Surprised, Abby mouths the words, "your babies" without saying them aloud.

Zack walks to the sliding glass door leading into the studio and taps on the glass. Beth rises from the mat on the floor where she has been sitting with the Twins and slides the door open.

Zack introduces Beth and Abby as they walk back to the mat.

"This is Julia and Nathan," Zack tells Abby as he kneels down to them on the mat. "They are the cutest babies on this planet."

Abby holds her finger out to Nathan and gives him a big smile.

"Indeed, they are," Abby says as she draws a smile from Nathan.

"How'd you do that?" Zack asks.

"Do what?" Abby responds.

"Get Nathan to smile," Zack replies.

"I think Nathan just knows a pretty girl when he sees one," Beth says with a laugh.

"Pay no attention to this Julia," Nathan says as he picks her up. "Your brother has a pretty girl with him all the time and is just too silly to realize it."

They play with Twins for a few minutes before Beth says, "I've got to put them down for their naps." "May I help?" Abby asks.

"Sure," Beth replies," I usually have help but Mondays are one of Arlette's days off."

Zack hands Julia to Beth as Abby picks up Nathan.

"I'll go get Abe moving," Zack says rising and disappearing out the door as Beth and Abby head to the nursery.

Zack walks to Abe's in-law suite and knocks on the glass.

"Be out in a minute," Abe says, "I just got myself tied up on a call with Steve DeJean."

Zack walks back to the patio table and sits down. Abby and Beth come out on the patio before Abe appears. Abby slides her chair closer to Zack's and takes his hand into hers as she sits down.

Abe comes out of his sliding glass door. Abby and Zack rise from the table.

"Abe," Zack says," this is Abby Phillips."

"At last," Abe says extending his hand and smiling broadly, "the elusive Ms. Phillips.'

"Abby," Zack says gesturing toward Abe, "this is my mentor and friend, Abe Stolz."

Abby shakes Abe's hand and gives him her most engaging smile.

"RJ tells me that you are a wizard," Abby says.

Abe laughs, "Some wizard. I couldn't even get my microwave to work right this morning."

They take their seats as Abby hands out the croissants and pastries.

"I'm glad to see that you two have finally caught up with each other," Abe says.

"I thinks it is more like I finally caught up with RJ," Abby says leaning her head on to Zack's shoulder.

"Well in any case," Abe says, "I'm really glad to see that the two of you have stopped running away from each other."

Both Zack and Abby grin sheepishly as Beth pours out coffee and tea.

"What do you do when you are not running away from Zack?" Abe asks with a twinkle in his eye.

"I'm finishing up a master's degree in fine arts at the Coventry Conservatory," Abby replies. "I will graduate on May 23rd."

"Any plans after that?" Abe asks.

"I'll probably teach for a year or two somewhere," Abby says as leans toward Zack, "but to be honest, my primary focus is going to be figuring out exactly where RJ and I stand."

"Won't that be rather difficult if you are over in Coventry and Zack is on the Island?" Beth asks.

"I'm hoping not," Abby says. "RJ is coming over to Coventry with me this afternoon and will stay until Wednesday morning. Normally I only have classes Tuesday through Friday at noon, so I'll come out here over the weekends. If we can keep to that schedule until school finishes next month, I think we will be fine."

They munch on the pastries for a few minutes before Abe says to Zack, "You said that you are going to show me what you are thinking of doing with that Tweed Connor verse."

"Let me go grab my tablet and I will show you," Zack says rising and walking to Abby's car where he pulls the tablet out of his backpack which he has packed for the trip to Coventry.

Abe rises from his chair saying, "Excuse me, I need to go in and get my notes. Without notes my brain no longer works."

Beth turns to Abby and says, "So you met Zack at the Hanover Conservatory?"

"I did," Abby replies. "We played together in a string quartet. Unfortunately, both of us were too young to realize that we were dealing with forces well beyond our control at that time."

"Do you still play?" Beth asks.

"I'm playing cello in a string ensemble at the moment," Abby replies. "I'm also trying to teach myself how to play piano on the side."

"Do you have anyone teaching you?" Beth asks.

"No," Abby says, "I've been trying to learn on my own. If I'm being honest with myself, I started trying to learn the piano to try to stop myself thinking about RJ so much."

"Would you like to come show me where you are?" Beth asks, motioning toward the studio. "I've finally gotten my grandmother's piano back and I've been dying to show it off to someone."

"Sure," Abby says rising from her chair and following Beth into the studio.

Zack returns with his tablet and sits back down in his chair. Abe comes out of his suite a few moments later carrying his tablet, some printouts and two green journals. The sound of Bach's Brandenburg concerto can be heard coming from the studio.

"Are you still thinking on working on a folk/sea song album with your father?" Abe asks.

"I'd like to," Zack says. "Problem is that lately, to my surprise, I keep finding myself writing blues songs."

"You think that will continue now that you have reconnected with Abby?" Abe asks.

"TBD, I'd think," Zack says with a shake of his head.

"I'm hoping that you are going into this thing with Abby with your eyes wide-open," Abe replies. "Sometimes the second falls can be worse than the first.

"I think that I am," Zack replies, "but to be honest, being with Abby is something I simply cannot stop myself from wanting."

Hoping to change the subject, Zack slides the laptop over to Abe. "Let me show you what I've got so far."

Abe studies what Zack has put together.

"I seem to be getting stuck on some of the language," Zack says. "I'm not sure whether I should change out words so people can understand them better. In all honesty, I'm not sure that I understand how all the words are used in that verse."

"I think in a lot of cases with folk and sea songs, it is more the matter of how the words sound than their actual meaning." Abe comments.

"I'm not sure how some of the words are supposed to sound," Zack says to Abe. "Would you mind reading it to me?"

Molly and Beth return from the studio.

"This girl can really play piano," Abby comments in reference to Beth as she sits back down beside Zack.

"You will get there," Beth responds to Abby. "You keep practicing, and you'll catch up to me in no time."

Abe sifts through his papers and finds Tweed Conner. He reads the entire poem in his rich Wannasea accent. While he has been reading, Zach has been furiously making notes in his tablet on the way Abe is pronouncing the words in question.

"That was a real treat, Abe," Abby says when Abe has finished. "Do you have something else which you might be able to read us?"

Zack and Beth look at each other, then both roll their eyes skyward.

Abe goes into his journal and selects a page one quarter of the way through it.

"Let's try 'Thomas Wanna's Sea'," Abe says.

Abe takes a sip of his tea before he reads the poem to Abby's rapt attention.

"That's almost better than music," Abby tells Abe. "I think that I could listen to it all morning."

After recognizing that Abby has now taken Abe captive, Zack glances at his watch which reads 10:55.

"I'm afraid we are going to have to run," Zack says. "I have to be down at Olivia's by 11:15 to sign off on the purchase of the SouthTown studio."

"We need to do this again soon," Beth says as she begins clearing the dishes.

Abby rises from her seat and goes to Beth and gives her a hug. She then walks to Abe and gives him a peck on his right check.

"Thanks so much," Abby says. "This is the best Monday morning which I've ever had."

Zack picks up his tablet from the patio table before taking Abby's hand and walking back to the Mini.

Zack stows his tablet in the backpack before starting up the car and heading toward Wannasea Village.

As they exit the traffic circle toward the Village, Abby asks, "Is the reason that you are trying to do this folk album simply because you want to do something with your dad?"

"That's a big part," Zack replies. "My dad isn't getting any younger. I don't know how much longer he and my Uncle Gene are going to be up to it."

"Seems to me your problem is going to be that you don't really seem all that interested in writing sea songs," Abby says.

"You're probably right," Zack says "but the only alternative would be to ask Abe to write the lyrics. The reality is that Abe's too busy with the Wannasea Historical Society to have any time for that."

"Why don't you just record Abe reciting the poems in that Island accent of his," Abby says. "You, your dad, and uncle can produce and play background music. You could donate the recordings to the Historical Society in your dad's name."

"That's not a bad idea," Zack says smiling. "I will ask my dad and see what he thinks about the idea."

Zack drives down MainStreet and pulls the Mini into the parking garage. They exit the garage and walk a block and half up the street to the Stolz law offices. The receptionist shows them into a large conference room. Abby and Zack have only been there for a few minutes before Olivia comes in carrying a stack of papers related to the purchase. Zack introduces Abby and Olivia before sitting down beside Abby and beginning to sign papers where Olivia has annotated them.

"Let me get Angelique," Olivia says. "I need her to witness the signing of the deed and land contract." Olivia disappears down the hallway and reappears in a few minutes with her sister.

It takes five more minutes of signing before Abby and Zack are out of the office and on their way to Coventry.

After they have left, as Olivia collects the signed papers, Angelique turns to her sister and says, "Do you have any idea, who the woman with Zack is?"

"Zack said her name is Abby," Olivia replies.

"That is Abigail Phillips," Angelique says. "Heiress to the Halifax Shipbuilding fortune. The last I'd heard, she is engaged to Alex Bougainville, an up-and-coming Hanover lawyer, who was just elected to the Hanover District Legislature last fall."

Return Path

Wednesday, April 23, 2:42PM. Zack is seated on an empty bench at the rear of the ferry. After two days spent in Coventry with Abby, he is on his way back to the Island. Abby had dropped Zack at the train station a little before 11. The train ride took two hours to get to Halifax. From the Halifax train station, Zack had taken a cab to the ferry dock.

On the entire trip, not one person has come up to Zack and asked him for an autograph, conversation, or anything else. This is due in large part to the help which Abby has given Zack in disguising himself. Zack is now the proud owner of two wigs, a short blond model and a rust-colored one with curls which he currently has on under the thin, hooded workout jacket which now covers his head. He also sports a new pair of large thick sunglasses. Zack had never felt so happy to go unrecognized.

The past five days with Abby had brought other surprises. Almost from the moment when Abby had shown up at his trailer door, Zack had begun to wonder how soon it would be before Abby reconsiders and bolts back to her fiancée and her gilded, settled life. Over the past four days, Abby has given Zack reasons to question this initial reaction.

During the weekend on the island with Abby, Zack had learned that Abby had not had a much easier time of it than he had after they were separated from each other 7 years ago. Abby had spent the better part of the first 18 months in spells of depression. She spent a solid year actively contemplating suicide. Abby had been basically just going through the motions until her final year at the university. Abby fell into a pattern of doing exactly what was expected of her. Her engagement seems to have been more an extension of Abby doing the expected to please her family than Abby having been excited by the prospect of marriage to Alex Bougainville.

Abby had started seeing her fiancée during the summer between her third and final year in Leeds. Twenty months later, Abby did the expected and accepted the marriage proposal which had been offered her. By that time, Abby had convinced herself that Zack was either dead or gone forever from her life. Her thinking had suddenly changed one spring day over two years ago, when Abby happened upon RJ in the main park in Hanover near the Medical Facility sitting on a bench playing a song on his guitar. After taking a few minutes to verify that it was indeed RJ seated on the bench, Abby had cautiously sauntered twenty feet closer and then moved behind a large bush which was behind RJ. She had peered through the branches and listened to him play Darius Rucker's "Don't Think I Don't Think About It". The song had been Clint Chadwick's favorite. From that moment, Abby not only began to keep tabs on RJ, but she also began to become less and less interested in doing the expected. She had sent her friends to Dave's when she discovered that RJ was working there. She had gone to Dave's once to see him play for herself. When Zack moved to 'The Place', there had seldom been a month that went by when either Abby herself or one of her friends didn't take in one of Zack Tillerman's performances or keep an eye on his comings and goings.

Abby had told Zack that at the end of last year, she knew that it was time to break off her engagement. She had tired of her fiancée's increasing possessiveness. Abby began to believe that in the eyes of her fiancée, she had become little more than a marriage trophy designed to increase his wealth and aid his political ambitions. At the Christmas break, Abby began pushing her fiancée to change their wedding date. First to the fall, then indefinitely. Her fiancée became ever more controlling and confrontational.

By February, Abby had decided that after her graduation, she was going to take direct action to determine exactly what if anything was left between Zack and herself. Abby told Zack that when she had come out to the beach in February, she had already made up her mind that the moment things were finished with her graduate degree in Coventry, Abby was calling of the engagement then coming to island to live for a while. Abby then planned to do everything in her power to either reconnect or permanently disconnect from Zack.

Her fiancée's increasing aggressive possessiveness and jealousy had sped up that decision. Last Friday, Abby had run out of tolerance for continuing to do the expected. Abby got angry and told Alex Bougainville exactly what he did not want to hear. When Alex became threatening, Abby threw his engagement ring at him. Abby then decided that she could not wait one moment longer to go out to the island and figure out her feelings for Zack.

Although Zack's mind and heart have been racing since last Friday night, it has been a long time since Zack has felt as rested and in control of himself as he is at this moment. As it had been almost seven years ago, being with Abby calmed him. He'd even enjoyed the two days spent with Abby and her two roommates in Coventry. When he kissed Abby goodbye at the Coventry train station, he felt as if for the first time in seven years, he was now able to fully breathe. Zack also knows as he sits on the ferry bench that he has placed himself in great emotional jeopardy. Emotionally Zack is now uncertain that he can afford to lose Abby for a second time.

As the ferry positions itself against the Wannasea pier, Zack pulls on his backpack and heads to the exit by the right front rail.

Zack walks quickly off the ferry. As he moves across the street, Zack notices a group of New Jericho Temple protestors lined up near where the vehicles enter the ferry. Most of the protestors are carrying signs which say, "Free the Prophet. Restore God's Dominion". He also hears the familiar sound of his song "New Jericho - Same Old Hate" coming from the record store across the street. Zack wonders if the resurgence of New Jericho protestors has been the driver for increased calls by the crowd to have the song played during his Wednesday performances. Zack decides to ignore the commotion and climbs into one of the waiting cabs parked along main street. He gives the cabby the address for his trailer park. Zack is once again surprised that the cabbie doesn't give him a second glance. As the cabbie drives toward the south part of the island, Zack pulls his cell phone out of his jacket pocket and texts Abby.

"Back on the island. Headed to do laundry. I miss you already."

Zack puts the cell phone back into his pocket and watches the familiar scenery pass until the cab reaches his trailer. As he pays for the cabbie, his cell phone buzzes. He pulls the phone from his pocket and before walking onto the deck, looks at Abby's reply.

"I miss you more. Call me after 5. Have a break from classes then."

As Zack walks across the deck to his front door, he notices that there are printed messages taped to the two windows of the door as well as the large front window of the living room. The messages are printed in large block letters and have been attached to his trailer with tape.

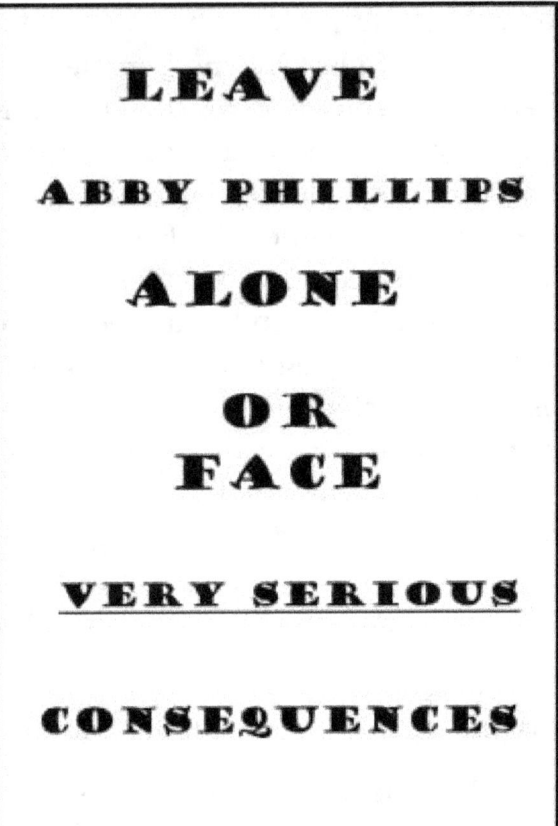

Zack unlocks the door to his trailer. He pulls off his backpack and places it on the couch before walking into the second bedroom and pulling three sheets of blank printer paper from the printer's tray. Zack walks back to out the front door of his trailer and pulls the three messages from the windows. As he does this, he attaches each of the messages to a blank piece of paper. He carries the pages to his bedroom and puts them atop the shelf over the clothes rack. He then walks to his dresser and pulls out two changes of clothes which he carries to the living room. He sets them on the couch while he pulls his worn clothes out of his backpack. Zack carries the dirty clothes back to the laundry room and puts them into an already half full laundry bag.

Zack had been planning on doing his laundry at the trailer. He decides perhaps that is not a prudent course of action at this point. Zack goes out of the trailer and walks around the right corner to the shed in back. He opens the shed and wheels his Vespa to the driveway after relocking the shed. Zack goes into the trailer, puts the clean clothes into his backpack. He then slings both the backpack and laundry bag over his back. He locks the trailer, goes to his scooter and heads toward the SouthTown studio.

'Going to have to watch my back for a while,' Zack decides as he turns left on South Mountain Way.

Over the three minutes it takes him to reach Southtown, Zack decides that he will have to make extra effort not to be where people expect him to be over the next few weeks. He pulls into the dry cleaners just three stores down from the studio and drops off the clothes to be laundered. Zack then parks the Vespa in front of the entrance to Dave's audio store. Dave looks at Zack warily for a few minutes before determining that it is Zack under the hoodie, curls, and sunglasses.

"Hey stranger," Dave, who is working the front counter says. "Where have you been?"

"I was over in Coventry for a few days," Zack replies.

"You mean to tell me that you actually left this island?" Dave says in mock amazement.

"I did," Zack says, "and I actually enjoyed every minute of it. Even got a chance to work out some of the details for our June concert while I was there. They are going to contact you about what audio equipment we want set up."

Although Zack is throwing out this information to avoid having to disclose more to Dave, it is not a lie. On Tuesday while Abby had been in class, Zack had gone to the Coventry base to discuss planning for the concert with two of Major Wallace's assistants.

"What's with the get up?" Dave asks, referring to Zack's disguise.

"Believe it or not," Zack replies, "this stuff works pretty well for warding off autograph seekers and agents."

"It fooled me for a minute," Dave comments.

"Do you mind if I put my Vespa inside the storeroom for a few days?" Zack asks.

Dave laughs, "In case it's escaped your attention, you are the owner of this place. You can do any darned thing you want here."

Zack walks out of the store and wheels the Vespa around to the storage room entrance. He lifts the scooter over the entrance and moves it into the corner away from the door. Noticing that there are two quilted moving blankets on the shelf beside it, Zack pulls one down and drapes it over the scooter. Zack walks out of the storage area and wheels one of the desk chairs into the recording studio, closing the door behind him.

Zack pulls off his backpack and sets it on the floor. He walks to the back wall and picks up his oldest acoustic guitar before returning to the chair and sitting down in it. He pulls his tablet out. Glancing at his wristwatch off and on, Zack spends the next hour and half working on refining the melody for 'rain keeps on fallin'.

Promptly at 5:05PM, Zack pulls out his cell phone and calls Abby,

She answers on the first ring. "Hi honey," Zack says, "how were your classes?"

"Boring," Abby replies, "I'm in the grind-it-out phase of higher learning. I'm also having some trouble stopping myself from thinking about you."

"Not having second thoughts, I hope," Zack says before he is able to restrain himself. He is instantly filled with regret for saying the words.

"I'm way past second thoughts," Abby replies. "I'm into the why-does-it-feel-so-bad when you aren't here with me phase,"

"If it helps you out," Zack says, "I'm in the same frame of mind."

"Just remember that when one of your cute fans starts coming on to you," Abby says.

"I'm not sure that I need to worry about that anymore," Zack replies. "Believe it or not the entire trip back to the island, nobody bothered me. People acted as if I weren't even there."

"See how much you need to have me around," Abby says with a laugh.

"Reality is," Zack replies, "during the train ride back to Halifax, I realized after that the first time we kissed in the practice room at Hanover Conservatory when we were sixteen, I have not stopped being in love with you. When they kicked me out of the Conservatory, I still loved you. When I was sent flying face first into the Iraqi desert, I loved you. When I was making crappy music over in Halifax, I loved you. Before you came to my door last Friday, I still loved you. What's more than a little frightening at the moment is that after five days with you, I'm certain that I love you even more."

Abby is silent for almost a full minute before responding, "I had similar thoughts when I was driving over to the island last Friday. I swear to you that I'm not going to allow anyone to keep us apart unless it's our own decision."

"For me, I'm not really sure that it is a decision," Zack replies. "It's like breathing, wanting to be with you is something I can't stop voluntarily."

"Seems to be the same here," Abby says. "Believe me RJ, I'm going to do everything I can to make certain that it stays that way."

"I'm reworking that song that I played you on Friday," Zack says. "Do you have time for me to play it for you?"

"I've got about five minutes before I need to head off to rehearsal," Abby replies.

Zack plays the song for her. "I'm trying to figure out whether or not to do the song with the band," Zack says after he completes the song.

"I like it acoustic," Abby replies. "Might not hurt to have a little bass and light percussion but I think that it is meant to be acoustic."

"Maybe you can help me fool around with it when you get here on Friday," Zack suggests.

"I'd like that," Abby says. "Listen I've got to scoot. I love you, RJ. Call me after your performance tonight. I don't care how late it is."

"I'll always love you Abby," Zack responds.

He waits until Abby disconnects the call before putting his cell phone into his windbreaker's pocket.

Mending Fences

Thursday, April 24, 10:12AM. Zack is astride his Vespa on his way from the SouthTown Studio to Mountain Village. After spending two hours on the phone with Abby last evening after his performance, Zack had gone to the studio and slept on the couch in the control room. Upon waking up this morning and going through his messages, he realized that Molly had not tried to contact him since Saturday. Normally Molly was good for at least two phone calls and five text messages a day. Zack has decided that he needs to take steps to make certain that Molly doesn't disappear from his life. Zack has few true friends. Zack knows that at this moment, Molly is the truest.

Zack wheels the Vespa up Mountain Way toward 'The Place'. He swings past the driveway going to the turnoff for Mountain Village. He parks the Vespa in the rear of the Meeting Center loading area and walks around the building to the main entrance.

Annette is at the front counter dealing with reservations at the computer terminal. Zack, who has on his blond wig with hooded shirt pulled over his head and sunglasses, walks to the counter.

"May I help you?" Annette says.

Zack takes off his sunglasses.

Annette studies him for a long moment before saying uncertainly, "Zack?"

"I am," Zack says with a big smile.

"That's quite the git-up that you have on," Annette says with a laugh.

"It works in preventing long lines of autograph seekers," Zack replies.

"What can I do for you?" Annette asks.

"First, I'm wondering if I can buy a pass to use the shower, restroom and laundry area?" Zack asks. "I'm having some work done at my trailer which has shut down my bathroom. If need be, I may need to rent one of the cabins for a month or so."

"Why don't you just get a membership at the new Aquatic Center," Annette asks. 'The facilities in there are great and you can swim or workout as well?"

"Not sure that's a good idea," Zack says. "I don't think I can wear the wig, sunglasses, and hooded shirt into the swimming pool. If I don't, my workout likely will become signing autographs."

"Fair point," Annette says.

Annette fishes into the top desk drawer and pulls out a blank access card for Mountain Village. She processes the card for one of the single units which have not as yet been built.

"This will get you in," Annette says as she hands the card over to Zack. "I'll talk to Marie to see if there will be any charge for it."

"You're an angel," Zack says.

"Remember that when you make out your will," Annette says with a laugh.

"Is Molly in?" Zack asks.

"She's in her office," Annette says, "Do you want me to ring her?"

"Please don't," Zack says. "I'd like to sneak up on her if it's okay."

"It's okay with me," Annette says, "but I'll warn you, sneaking up on Molly these days may not be a good idea. She might just take your head off."

"I'll take my chances," Zack says as he puts his sunglass back on, walks across the lobby before climbing the stairs. He turns left and walks to the end of the hallway where Molly's office is. Molly is seated at her desk going over a printout of the May schedule for "The Shell".

Molly looks up at Zack in annoyance.

"Looking for something?" Molly asks with a tinge of hostility.

Zack takes off his sunglasses. It takes Molly a full 30 seconds to recognize that it is Zack. Despite herself, Molly bursts out laughing.

"What in God's name caused you to dress up like that?" Molly says through her fit of laughter.

"This way of dressing has reduced my contact with autograph seekers and agents by at least 90%," Zack says.

"Seriously?"

"Seriously," Zack replies.

"What brings you to my office?" Molly asks her demeanor suddenly returning to ice cold. "First I want to know why I haven't heard a word from you in five days," Zack replies pulling up the chair in front of her desk. "We are still partners."

Molly narrows her eyes.

"Business partners."

"Are you mad at me?" Zack asks.

"No, I'm not mad at you, Zack," Molly replies with her eyes now cast downward. "I'm mad at me. Mad that I could have been such a damned fool to think there would ever be anything more between us than business."

"Knock it off, Molly," Zack says. "There's always been more between us than business. From where I sit, you remain one of the best friends I have in my life. I'm here to try to make certain that doesn't end."

Molly looks up at Zack with tears beginning to come into her eyes.

"Please don't cry, Molly," Zack says. "I'm not worth the tears."

"I'm not crying for you," Molly says angrily. "I'm crying for me."

Molly pulls a tissue from the container on her desk and dabs her eyes.

"I went over to Coventry earlier this week and checked out the venue," Zack says as he fishes into his wallet to pull out two business cards. "Here are the cards for the two people who I met. They asked if you'd give them a call to firm things up.

Zack places the cards on the table just above the printouts which Molly had been reviewing.

"I've also made a commitment to do the tour in December," Zack says. "I'll be leaving on the 27th of November and won't get back until December 19th. I talked with the NorthEnders and they said they can't commit. In fact, Jerome said that they want to use this summer to see if they can get anywhere on their own. After June, we may need to look for a new band."

Molly blows her nose then takes out another clean tissue and dabs her eyes again. She tosses the tissues into the wastebasket beside her desk.

"Zack," Molly says looking up and directly into Zack's eyes, "you've been honest with me from the start. I cannot blame you for leading me on. The leading on, I did to myself. You are however going to have to understand that I need some time to think things through."

"Does that mean that you aren't going to speak with me for a while?" Zack asks.

"I'm not going to speak with you when she is around," Molly says. "Otherwise, I'll try to get back to business."

"I'm hoping that includes continuing to be my friend," Zack says.

"I can't promise you that right now, Zack."

Zack studies Molly for a few moments, realizing that he has taken this as far as he can for the time being.

"Is there anything that you need from me?" Zack asks.

"I've got some checks that I need to get to you, but I probably won't have them ready until later on in the afternoon," Molly says. "I'd also like to know what you are going to be recording so I can project our costs."

"We will do some recordings of Abe's poems with a light folk background over the next month or so," Zack replies. "I've decided to give up on making a new folk album. I'm just not into it. Instead, my dad and I have decided to produce recordings of Abe reciting the history of Wannasea Island from both his verses and the verses in his grandmother's journals. When finished, the recordings will be donated to the Historical Society. I'm willing to pay for the recordings out of my own pocket if you don't want to do it through ZackTillerman."

"Using ZackTillerman is better," Molly says sitting herself more upright. "I kind of like the idea of making those recordings. Abe's not getting any younger, you know."

Zack nods his head in agreement, "I'm going over to do planning with him right after this. I'm hoping we can use 'The Place' on Monday evenings for the next couple months to make those recordings."

"I already spoke with Beth about it," Molly replies. "I've blocked out all the Mondays for the rest of April, May, and June to record. Beth and Marie also told me that there would be no charge for using the facility."

"That's wonderful," Zack replies.

"I think you ought to talk with Beth while you are over there," Molly says. "I think she would like to help you out with background music."

"Did she say that means she'd play the piano for us," Zack asks.

"I think it does," Molly replies, "but you really should talk to her."

"Guess I've taken up enough of your time," Zack says. "I'll swing by later this afternoon to pick up the check."

Molly looks up from her desk.

"Thanks Zack."

"Thank you, Molly," Zack says as he rises, dons his sunglasses and heads out of Molly's office.

Zack waves to Annette, who is tied up with a couple customers, as he goes past the counter on his way out of the Meeting Center. He walks around the building. Picks up his helmet off the Vespa's seat, fires the scooter up and drives down to Beth & Abe's house. Zack sees that Abe's car isn't in the parking lot. He spots Beth seated at the kitchen table working on her laptop. He knocks lightly on the sliding glass door to the kitchen. Beth gets up and lets Zack in.

"Just catching up on council work," Beth says by way of explanation.

"Molly said that you want to talk to me about possibly helping my dad and I come up with the background music for Abe's recordings," Zack says.

"I would," Beth replies, "that and one other thing."

"Okay," Zack says hesitantly. "Let's talk music first."

"I'd like to work out being your piano player and helping arrange the music," Beth says.

"That would be great," Zack says. "Maybe you and I could start a little before the sessions which are planned to start at six?"

"I can do that if there aren't any unscheduled council meetings," Beth replies. "Right now, the council sessions are Tuesday through Thursday so I should be okay."

"Wonderful," Zack replies. "I can't start doing the sessions until May 7th. I've got some things which I need to do with Abby until then. Until the end of May, my being able to attend will depend on Abby."

"I'm fine with that," Beth says. "Actually, Abby is the other thing which I want to talk with you about."

Zack looks at Beth curiously.

"I know that Abby seems to be a lovely person," Beth says. "It's easy to see why you are head-over-heels with her, but I think you may be playing with fire."

"Honestly Beth," Zack says, "not having Abby in my life has been the playing with fire part."

"Olivia told me that Abby is not only the sole heir to one of the largest fortunes on the Mainland," Beth says, "but that she is engaged to a very powerful young man from Hanover. Where I come from that spells trouble with a capital T."

Zack is caught somewhat off-guard by Beth's reference to "largest fortune". Zack knows Abby comes from serious money. Up until this moment, Zack had no idea that Abby was the sole heir to a fortune. Zack's not sure he has any interest in being caught up in fortunes.

Over the next thirty minutes Zack explains in detail his history and the current situation with Abby.

When Zack has finished, Beth looks at him with worried eyes, "I knew that you've led a somewhat complicated life. Seems that I had no idea how complicated."

"Complicated is one way to put it," Zack replies.

"I just want to make certain that you know exactly what you have gotten yourself into," Beth says. "This island needs you. Your family needs you. My family needs you."

"I've gone into this thing with my eyes wide open," Zack says to Beth. "What I can tell you is not being with Abby is not an option for me, right now."

The Calm

Thursday, April 24, 1:14PM. Zack has ridden over to Halifax with Dave, who is picking up some new audio equipment. Zack has plans to meet Abby on her drive in from Coventry. She should be in Halifax by 2:30. Before then Zack had arranged to meet with Alfie at his apartment. Zack has come up with an idea for a song which he hopes that Alfie might consider recording.

Dave wheels his van into the parking lot behind a row of shops. Alfie shares a flat over those shops with two of her working companions. Alfie, who Zack had just texted three minutes ago is standing at the bottom of the stairs which leads to the apartment. Zack, in wig, hooded shirt and sunglasses, opens the door of the van with his tablet and a manilla folder in hand.

"Thanks for the ride," Zack says to Dave as he climbs out.

"See you back on the Island," Dave replies before pulling away.

"That's some fashion choice," Alfie says with a laugh. "I'm not sure if it's late-stage Justin Bieber or Britney Spears' ex."

"Whatever you call it," Zack says. "It's very effective in avoiding autograph seekers and agents."

Alfie leads Zack up the stairs and into the apartment where the lady, who had performed as Cher, is seated at their small kitchen table."

"Welcome to my castle," Alfie says.

The Cher impersonator says, "I see that you just couldn't stay away from me."

Zack laughs.

"I'm sure you remember Cheri Pie," Alfie says as she pulls out the chair at the end of the table for Zack to sit. "What have you got?"

Zack hands Alfie the manila folder which contains copies of the lyrics and melody from song which he has been working on that he is calling "Cross Dressin'". Cheri Pie rises from her chair and goes to where Alfie now sits and looks over his shoulder.

"He's not only cute," Cheri Pie says to Alfie, "he's talented."

"Before we get into that," Alfie says to Zack, "I've got something I want to show you."

Alfie gets up from the table and walks into the main room. He picks up an acoustic guitar which is beside the sofa. He walks back to the wide entrance to the kitchen and breaks into the opening stanza of 'Don't Blame it on the Alcohol'. Zack is stunned by how much Alfie sounds like his first recording of the song.

"When did you learn to play guitar?" Zack asks Alfie.

"I dabbled with it a little back on the Island," Alfie discloses. "I'm now spending 3 hours a day with a guy named Earl Evans learning how to play.

Zack recalls the name "Earl Evans" from his days in Halifax playing at 'Dave's'.

"Is that the same Earl Evans, who used to play with "Los Diablos"?" Zack asks.

"Yes," Alfie replies. "He's retired now. I talked to him at the bar the first week that I was here. He started giving me lessons three weeks ago."

"Either he's a hell of a teacher," Zack replies, "or you are a guitar playing savant."

Alfie reddens slightly before taking the guitar back into the living room, setting it down then returning to the table to look at the contents of Zack's folder. For the next hour, they work on refining the song which Zack has brought. Alfie sings parts of it. Zack makes notes on his tablet. All the while encouraging Alfie to come up with a few more songs to record. Zack is lost in the music when his cell phone buzzes. It's Abby. 'I'm just a couple minutes away," Abby announces.

"I'll come out to meet you," Zack replies. "Call me if you have any trouble finding the place."

Zack picks up his laptop and rises from the kitchen chair.

"Why don't you come down and meet Abby?" Zack suggests. "I think we should," Cheri Pie replies. "I always like to check out my competition."

Zack follows Alfie down the stairs with Cheri Pie in tow. They are only there for a few moments before Abby's Mini appears. Abby parks it about ten feet from them and exits the car.

As Abby walks toward them, Cheri Pie turns toward Zack and whispers, "You have very good taste in women."

Abby tightly embraces Zack and gives him a hungry kiss. After Zack and Abby have moved apart a little, he walks her over to Alfie and Cheri Pie.

"Abby," Zack announces, "this is Alfie and Miss Cheri Pie."

Abby reaches out her hand and gives both ladies a big smile as she shakes their hands.

"Ladies," Zack replies, "this is Abby Phillips."

"Zack tells me you have quite the voice," Abby says to Alfie.

Alfie blushes before saying, "I can sing a little."

"I'm going to Germany in couple of weeks," Abby says. "Would you sing part of that Marlene Dietrich song which Zack told me about?"

"I'm not sure I can do it here," Alfie says reddening.

"Put on your big girl pants," Cheri Pie advises Alfie. "Sing the song for Zack's lady."

Alfie focuses himself for a moment, before breaking into a pitch perfect version of "Lili Marleen" in German. Abby's jaw has dropped precipitously.

"Wow," Abby says. "Just wow."

"He's got to get himself recorded," Zack injects.

"Indeed," Abby.

Zack walks closer to Alfie and Cheri Pie, "We are going to have to get going. Thanks for the hospitality." "Anytime," Cheri Pie replies. "When are you coming back out to see us?"

"Soon," Zack replies.

"He's going to have to wait until I can come with him," Abby adds. "I have to see you perform."

They walk with Zack and Abby to the car.

"You drive," Abby says to Zack. "You know where we are going."

Zack had promised to take Abby to get halibut before heading to the Island.

Zack swings into the driver's seat and calls back to Alfie, "Work on the song and let me know when you are ready to record."

Cheri Pie walks with Abby to the passenger side of the Mini and holds the door open for her as she climbs inside.

"Miss Abby, I hope that you know what a very lucky lady you are," Cheri Pie says to Abby.
"I do know," Abby replies.

"We are counting on you to take care of him," Cheri Pie says before closing the door.
"I will," Abby says softly as Zack starts up the Mini and they wave goodbye to the pair.

Zack maneuvers the vehicle east a few blocks before Abby says, "I think that Miss Cheri Pie has eyes for you."

Zack laughs, "Are you jealous?"

"Maybe," Abby says, "Should I dye my hair black to make you forget about her?"

"Don't you dare," Zack says with a laugh.

Abby takes Zack's hand into both of hers, as Zack negotiates the few miles to the parking lot for the restaurant. After they have gone into the restaurant, which has only two more customers, Zack pulls down the hoodie, pulls off the sunglasses and the wig.

"Hey stranger," Abby says sideling close to him and buzzing his cheek.

After placing their order, signing autographs for four members of the restaurant staff, Abby says, "Before we get back into making up for lost time, I think that we need to discuss necessities and unwanted realities. Which do you want to deal with first?"

"I'll take unwanted realities," Zack replies.

"I spoke with my mom for a long while last night after I talked to you," Abby says.

"What did your mom have to say?" Zack asks.

"That she wasn't really all that surprised that I broke off the engagement with Alex," Abby says.

"That's interesting," Zack replies uncertain if it really is.

"She's also certain that I am now going through a phase," Abby replies. "She and my dad feel that if they give me enough time, I will come to what they are calling "my senses"._

"I see," Zack said. "What did you say to that?"

"I told Mom that I have finally come to my senses after seven years," Abby replies squeezing Zack's hand. "I also told her that she had best be preparing herself for what she is calling a "phase" to last the rest of her life."

Zack sincerely hopes that Abby is right.

"You'll get a kick out of what Mom said about Alex," Abby says. "She said that Alex had become "extremely unctuous" over the past year and was not all that sorry that I'd cut him loose."

"I don't know anything about this Alex guy," Zack says, "but "extremely unctuous" seems a strange choice of words."

"It wouldn't be if you knew my mother," Abby says. "After I thought about it for a while, I also realized that my mother's opinion is spot on."

"I'll take necessities next," Zack says hoping to change the subject.

"First," Abby says, "I want to go with you on this trip that for Military in December. I'm not spending almost a month without you."

"I will speak with Major Wallace about it," Zack says. "You might have to play violin or piano for me if you come."

"I'd be okay with that," Abby replies, "but I don't want you just to talk with the Major. I want you to tell her that my coming is non-negotiable."

"All right," Zack says.

"Next," Abby says, "In a month I will be finished with school. We need to figure out our living arrangements by then."

"You can always live with me in my trailer," Zack says with a big smile.

Abby narrows her eyes and gives him an are-you-are-out-of-your-damned-mind look.

"It was just a thought," Zack says in mock contrition.

"Right now," Abby says, "you shouldn't be living in that trailer. It's not safe. How long before some crazy fan busts in on you?"

"You're the only fan who has busted in on me so far," Zack says trying to suppress a laugh.

Abby's eyes narrow further.

"Be serious."

Zack leans over and kisses her on the cheek.

Abby shakes her head before saying, "I'm willing to come live with you on the Island, if you agree to move into the villa. My parents have not been to the villa in years. I already spoke with my mother about it. She said that she would be okay with our moving in there."

Zack fiddles with his glass of water for a few moments, before turning somber and saying, "Don't take this the wrong way, but I have a problem with living in a place which belongs to your parents."

Abby takes Zack's left hand which has been fiddling with the water glass and puts her hand over his.

"Believe me RJ, I understand that you have ample cause for not trusting my parents."

Abby rubs the fingers of Zack's hand for a few moments before saying, "What if I buy the villa off my parents?"

"Wouldn't that be pretty much the same thing?"

"No, it wouldn't," Abby says sternly. "I have my own money. My grandparents left me a trust fund. I would make certain that the property is transferred to me legally."

"I'd really prefer that we live somewhere that we both own," Zack replies. "Why don't we buy something together?"

"Why don't we buy the villa together?"

"Only if we can purchase it 50-50," Zack replies.

"That's going to be a pretty big chunk of money," Abby says.

"Last time I checked,' Zack responds, "money isn't my problem."

As their food arrives, Abby asks, "Is it okay if I ask my parents what price they might sell the villa to us for?"

"Okay," Zack replies, "but I'm expecting the price to be close to market value."

Abby leans over and kisses Zack on the cheek.

They spend the next 30 minutes eating and exchanging small talk before Zack puts the blond wig back on, pulls up the hoodie and dons his sunglasses.

During the trip to the Halifax peer to catch the ferry, Zack and Abby discuss Zack's plans to record Alfie. After they have entered the hold of the ferry and the boat leaves the pier, as they had done when they were teenagers, Zack and Abby make out during the entire trip to Wannasea Island.

Once out of the ferry, Zack drives the Mini to SouthTown and picks up his backpack before driving to Abby's parent's villa. After Zack has parked the Mini in the underground garage, Abby takes the keys and pops up the lid to the trunk which is full of packages.

"Help me," Abby says to Zack as she begins loading him down with packages to carry into the villa.

"What are all these?" Zack asks.

"You'll see," Abby replies as she leads him into her bedroom, where they place the packages atop Abby's dresser and the two chairs.

"Let's go for a swim," Abby says pulling off her peach-colored dress and begins looking in the drawers for her swimsuit.

Zack takes his well-worn swimsuit out of his backpack, along with the now clean panda t-shirt. He changes into them and follows Abby out to the pool after she has picked up three towels from the closet.

When they reach the edge of the pool, Abby moves beside of Zack and begins to pull his t-shirt up. "This comes off," Abby says.

Zack frowns and tries to tug his shirt back down.

"Stop it, RJ," Abby says stubbornly. "The shirt comes off."

Zack relents and Abby pulls the shirt up over his head. She kisses him after she has tossed the shirt on a pool chair. She reaches around and rubs Zack's scared back.

"That's our history written on your back," Abby says. "I don't ever want you hiding your back from me again."

Zack gives in and begins gradually backing into the pool with Abby kissing him and tenderly rubbing his scars. They swim for forty minutes then go back to the bedroom and spend an hour making love. After twenty minutes in the shower together, they begin grooming themselves, Abby leads Zack back into the bedroom and begins pulling men's clothes from the boxes on the dresser as Zack puts on underwear and socks.

She hands Zack a custom fitted pair of black jeans. Abby had managed to get the size exactly right. The jeans fit Zack's muscled body like a second skin.

Abby pulls a silver silk shirt from a box on the first chair.

"I like the silver shirt you usually wear on stage," Abby says, "but I think this silk one will look better." Zack puts on the shirt, after which Abby hands him a black belt with inlaid silver medallions.

"Now those deck shoes need to go," Abby says bring over a pair of just-above the ankle, midnight-black, lizard skin Tecovas boots.

Zack sits on the bed and pulls on a pair of thin black socks before putting on the boots. Abby comes to the bed and takes him by the hand, then leads him to the mirrors on the front wall.

"Damn," Abby says, "you look fine. Did you ever think that you could look this good?"

Zack looks at his image in the mirror, despite himself, Zack has to admit that Abby is right. What Zack normally wears to his performances compared to what he now has on, is like comparing the sweatsuit which he uses to disguise himself with a tuxedo.

"You're right," Zack says as walks away from the mirror and moves toward her. "Thanks for buying all this stuff but I'm now feeling bad that I didn't get you anything."

"You came out to Halifax to meet me when you've got better things to do," Abby says moving toward him and hugging him. "You brought me Alfie singing the Marlene Dietrich song. You bought me a great meal. You make me so happy that I can't get over it. That's more than an even trade."

The Expected Unexpected

Wednesday, April 29, 2:21PM. Zack climbs out of the cab which he had caught down in the village on his trip back from Coventry. He slides the driver a $20 bill and tells him to keep the change. He walks over to his battered VW which he'd parked ten days ago at the far eastern edge of the parking lot at 'The Place'. Zack has decided that it is time for the vehicle to be moved if it is going to serve as a diversion.

Zack unlocks the Bug and tosses his backpack into the back. He starts the engine without any trouble. The bug may be dinged and dented but it is still nothing else if not reliable. He swings out of the parking lot and goes down Mountain Way. He turns right at the roundabout and heads for his trailer. He needs to pick up his medications which had run out on Monday.

Zack wasn't going to be on the Island long. He was going back to Coventry to meet Abby on Friday to bring her back to Wannasea. She would stay until Saturday night, when Zack was planning to drive her back to Coventry to catch her Sunday flight to Germany. Abby was going to be in Germany performing for the next week.

Zack follows the familiar road to his trailer. He parks the Bug in front of the deck. He hops out to find that three new messages have been posted on his trailer.

> # LEAVE
>
> # ABBY PHILLIPS
>
> # ALONE
>
> ## Final Warning
>
> ## Injuries will follow

Zack pulls the two messages from the windows on his trailer door and places them back-to-back. He pulls the other message from the front window and carries them into the trailer. He walks into the kitchen and sets the messages on the counter before going to the refrigerator and pulling out a bottle of water. Zack uncaps it and takes a swallow before walking out of the kitchen area into the bedroom. He goes to the dresser, pulls out two changes of clothes and his medications which he carries into the living room area and sits down on the couch. Deciding that he will need his suitcase for the coming week, Zack walks back out the trailer's front door.

Zack's chest is immediately met by the fist of a small burly man, who before Zack has said a word has punched him again in the right eye area. Zack sees stars and can immediately feel his eye beginning to swell. Ignoring the pain, like a cat, Zack jumps toward the right side of his trailer. He tosses the contents of his water bottle at the man's face to distract him. The man, who is much slower, moves toward him. Zack positions himself and kicks the man directly in the stomach, knocking him against the side of trailer and creating a rather sizeable dent. The kick has knocked the breath out of the man. Zack jumps to the left and sidekicks the man in the right rib area. Zack, surprised that the kick does not bring the man down, leaps behind his attacker and puts him in a 'Marine Chokehold' by reaching around the man with his left arm, putting the attacker's windpipe in the crook of his arm. Zack then places his left hand on the inside crook of his right elbow and pushes the man's head down hard with his right hand.

Zack begins counting, "One thousand one, On thousand two…"

By the time that Zack has reached one thousand nine, the man has slumped to the ground on his side.

Zack scurries to his shed and pulls out a package of ¼" wide, 18" long zip ties which he normally uses to secure music stands. He fashions two sets of tie-wrap handcuffs tightly around the man's hands. He then binds a tie wrap through the two sets of handcuffs and runs it through the belt loops on the front of the man's pants. He cinches the last tie wrap tight. Zack then makes a similar set of tie-wrap cuffs around the man's ankles leaving a 6" connection between the two ankles. Throughout the tie wrapping the man has not moved. Zack quickly goes through the unconscious man's pockets. He finds car keys, a switchblade in the right pocket and a set of metal knuckles in the left pocket. He pulls them out and puts them in his own front pocket. He then pulls the wallet out of the man's back pocket and slides the driver's license from it. Zack walks to his picnic table and takes two pictures of the license, front and back. Zack takes note of the man's name, "Michael Papadopoulos". Zack puts the license back into the wallet and returns it to his attacker's rear pocket. Zack, having become worried that he has gone too far with the chokehold, puts his finger on the man's nose to make certain that he is still breathing. Uncertain that he can detect anything, Zack rises and goes into the trailer. He fills a plastic pitcher full of cold water from the faucet, picks up a notepad and pen before returning to where the man lies.

Zack pulls up one of his patio chairs and places himself about five feet from the man. He throws half of the pitcher of water in the man's face. It takes approximately three seconds for the man's eyes to begin fluttering. Zack throws the remainder of the water into the man's face. He waits for the thirty seconds which it takes for the man to return to some semblance of consciousness.

As the man pulls himself into a sitting position on the deck and looks at Zack through glassy eyes, Zack pulls out his phone and dials all but the last digit of the number for the Constabulary.

"Here's the deal, Michael Papadopoulos," Zack says to the still groggy man. "Either you tell me the information which I want to hear or I'm going to finish this call to the Constabulary."

The man squeezes his eyelids narrow then winces.

"Where the hell did you learn that stuff?" his attacker asks incredulously.

"The Army," Zack replies. "I used to be an advanced scout for a motorized unit. Advanced scout being the name the Army uses for "chief ass-kicker and name taker" but we're not here to talk about me. We are here to either talk about you or have a visit from the local Constable. Which will it be?"

"What do you want to know," the man says still trying to clear his head.

"Who sent you?" Zack says gruffly.

"You don't seem to understand how this stuff works," the man replies. "I work for a guy, who does things for people. I have no idea who hired us. I just do what my boss tells me. In your case, my boss said that you are messing around with somebody's wife and it's time you stopped or get hurt."

"Abby Phillips is nobody's wife," Zack replies. "Abby Phillips is nobody's property. Understand?"

"That's not what I was told," the man replies.

"Well, you were told wrong," Zack replies. "Seeing as how you don't seem to know much; I'm going to give you something to do for me."

"I'm no errand boy," the man says angrily.

"You are if you don't want to spend a little time in the Wannasea jail," Zack replies.

"What do you want?" the man asks.

"I want you to go back to your boss," Zack begins, "and tell him that if he sends you or anyone else after me, I will do worse than I have just done to you to whoever he sends out next time. Then I'll come looking for him. If he won't tell me who has hired him, I'm going to use the same chokehold I just used on you and forget to let go of the hold when I reach ten. Capeesh?"

"I'll tell him, but it is going to result in your funeral."

Zack picks up the pen and writes, "Alex Bougainville" then "Halifax Shipbuilding" on the notepad. He tears off the sheet of paper, walks to the man and shoves it into his front shirt pocket.

"You can also tell him that I'm pretty sure that one of those two entities on that slip of paper is who hired you," Zack says. "Your boss needs to pass along to his customer that after I'm finished with him, I will come looking for them. That's a promise not a threat."

"You don't know who you are dealing with kid," Papadopoulos says. "These are some rough people."

"I've dealt with rougher people," Zack says. "People, who don't play by rules. They taught me how not to play by the rules."

Zack watches as the man tries to get up but is unable to establish enough balance to force himself upwards.

Zack walks to the shed, returns the unused tie-wraps and pulls down a 22" brown suitcase. He rolls the suitcase out of the shed then closes the door and locks it.

Zack returns to the man, who has scooted himself to the side of the trailer and is trying to bring himself erect by using the trailer as support. He is failing miserably.

Zack walks to his open front door and sets the suitcase inside before returning to the man. "You're just going to leave me here?" the man asks.

"That's a thought," Zack says, "but I'm in a good mood today."

Zack goes behind the man and grabs below his left arm to help him become erect.

"What about these," the man asks attempting to hold out his tie-wrapped hands to Zack.

"You seem resourceful," Zack says, "I'm sure you'll figure something out."

The man starts crab-walking across Zack's deck.

"If you haven't gotten yourself sorted out by the time that I head out in a few minutes," Zack says, "I'll drop your keys and knife off at your car. Where's it parked."

"Down at the beach parking lot," Papadopoulos says. "It's a silver four-door Ford."

"Be careful not to trip going down the hill to the beach," Zack calls out to the man as he watches him carefully move off the deck and down the driveway. "I'm not helping you up again."

Zack collects the pitcher, pad and pen and takes them back into the trailer. He sets them on the kitchen counter. Zack then goes to the freezer portion of his refrigerator and pulls out a pack of frozen peas which he presses against his right eye. He continues holding the package of peas in front of his throbbing right eye as he goes to the couch, picks up the clothing and medications and packs them into the suitcase. Zack rolls the suitcase out of the trailer. locks the trailer door, then still holding the peas to his eye, goes to his Bug and puts the suitcase in the trunk. Zack studies his right eye in the bug's rear-view mirror. It is dark red trending toward blue and swollen. The eye is going to look nasty for tonight's performance.

Zack fires up the engine and goes down the trailer park driveway still holding the peas to his eye. With his left eye, Zack sees Papadopoulos struggling to open the trunk of his car.

Zack pulls into the beach parking lot. He puts down the package of peas, pulls out his phone and notes the license number of Papadopoulos's vehicle into his current notepad. Zack then rolls down the driver's side window as he pulls up 10 feet behind Papadopoulos. Zack fishes the switchblade out of his pocket and tosses it a Papadopoulos's feet. "Don't forget to give your boss my message," Zack shouts out before puts the peas back against his eye and speeds out of the parking lot headed to 'The Place'.

Respite

Thursday, April 30, 8:01AM. Zack sits up in Abby's bed. Her alarm has just gone off, but Abby is already awake and, in the shower, preparing for her 9AM class.

During the phone call after his show last evening, Zack had told Abby about his right eye, which is now blackened and swollen shut, by saying that he'd had an incident with an overly aggressive fan at the trailer earlier in the day. He'd had to talk Abby out of driving out to Wannasea. He managed to calm her down by arranging to have the guard at the security gate drive him to Coventry late last night for the sum of $400. Zack had arrived at the house Abby shares with two other girls at 1:30AM.

After Abby had examined the condition of Zack's eye, she became even more worried about his current living arrangements.

Abby comes out of the bathroom wrapped in one towel and rubbing her long hair with another.

"You need to go back to sleep," Abby says. "I'll wake you up when I get back from class at 11."

Sleep wasn't exactly on Zack's mind. His sense of apprehension was growing by the second. Zack was now hearing Clint's voice saying, "There's trouble up ahead. Watch your back, kid."

Zack didn't want to admit that part of the reason that he'd decided to come to Coventry beyond tempering Abby's insistence to drive alone to Wannasea and pick him up, was his growing sense that he may no longer be safe on Wannasea Island.

Zack's first reaction to the messages posted on his trailer's windows had been to not take them all that seriously. Although

Zack had taken steps to make himself difficult to find, he'd felt the messages were too sophomoric to have been written by anyone capable of doing him serious harm. He still felt the messages were somewhat childish, but now knew whoever had hired Papadopoulos, was serious about having harm done to him. Zack's biggest worry had become that that person may well be Abby's father.

Abby sits down on the bed and leans against Zack's bare chest.

"That eye looks bad," Abby says. "You told me it was just a little bruise. That's a lot more than a little bruise, RJ."

"It really wasn't all that bad last night," Zack offers.

"Katy is going to run to the drugstore and get you something to put on it. I want you to promise me that you'll use it."

"Will do," Zack replies almost automatically.

"You also need to promise me when you are back on the Island," Abby says, "that you will not go near that trailer of yours. I'll get someone to clean it out. We'll have your stuff moved over to the Villa."

Zack doesn't know how to tell Abby that he's begun to fear that moving into the Villa is probably less safe than the trailer. At the trailer, it is hit or miss for someone coming after him. At the Villa, if Abby's father is the source of the Papadopoulos' attack, he's an easy mark. Zack is willing to risk his personal safety on his hunch that he won't be attacked when he is with Abby but decides he's going to have to figure out how to avoid being at the Villa when Abby is not there.

"Is there a way someone can get in your trailer if I send them there to clean your stuff out?" Abby asks.

"There's a key in the shed. I can tell them the code to get in." Zack says deciding that appeasement is the best option for the moment.

"Are you hungry?" Abby asks.

"Not really," Zack replies. "I think I'll take your advice and go back to sleep after you leave."

Abby stays leaning against Zack's chest and holding on to his right hand.

"I was going to tell you last night," Abby says, "but after seeing your eye, I was too upset. My mom told me that they are going to give me the Villa as a graduation present."

"I thought we agreed that we would buy it jointly?" Zack replies

"I think I've figured out how we can work that out," Abby says. "I've decided to try to create a symphony orchestra over on the Island. Beth put me in touch with the Lt. Governor to start working on it. We hope to start having Sunday concerts every other week starting in July. I'm in touch with the people at Island Resorts casino and they are willing to give us their event center a couple of times a month during the winter."

"What's that got to do with the Villa?" Zack interrupts.

"If you donate half of the appraised value of the Villa to the startup fund for the orchestra, I will have your name added to the deed," Abby says. "I've already spoken with the lawyers, and they see no problem with doing it that way."

Zack thinks for a long moment before say, "I guess that will work."

Zack hears Hiram's voice in his head, "Don't trust no one around here. The moment you start trusting is when they'll blow your ass up."

"You could also really make me happy if you'd agree to play with symphony when you have time," Abby says.

"I wouldn't mind that," Zack says vaguely. "It will be hard to pull off with my performance schedule, though."

"You can just do it once in a while," Abby says. "When it fits your schedule."

A knock comes on the bedroom door.

"I'll take you to lunch at 'The Grill' when I get back," Abby says before moving to the door.

"Abby?" they hear Katy's voice call.

Abby rises from the bed and opens the door a crack for Katy to hand her a tin of Arnica. "Tell Zack that I hope this helps," Katy says.

"I will," Abby says. "Thanks for running to get this. If I hadn't had to turn this damned thesis over to Culvert this morning, I would have gone myself. Do you have time to go to lunch with Zack and I at noon?"

"Sure," Katy replies. "I'll see you then."

Abby shuts the door, goes into the bathroom to get Q-tips then carefully applies the salve around Zack's eye.

"I think that I would have been a pretty good nurse," Abby says when she is finished with the application.

"I don't know about that," Zack says as he pulls Abby close to him and kisses her, "but I'm certain the majority of your male patients would certainly enjoy having you be their nurse."

"Did you do this to the nurses when you were in the hospital at Hanover?" Abby asks, pulling away from him as she notices that she is running out of time to get dressed for her class.

"Most of my nurses were male," Zack replies.

"Probably for good reason,' Abby replies as she moves from the bed and runs to her closet and begins dressing.

Zack can't stop himself from watching Abby get dressed in the mirror. It's a habit which began when Zack was 17. Zack truly believes that Abby dressing is a form of art as he watches her pull on a pair of stretch jeans and a flowery blouse.

"This is going to be a no makeup day," Abby announces as she slips on a pair of sandals.

She slides her laptop into its soft case then places her 254-page document on "The 17th Century Replacement of the Viola by Cello" into the separate side compartment.

"Get some sleep,' Abby says as she moves toward the door. "I love you, Ralph Jones."

"Bossy as you are, I love you too, Abigail,' Zack replies. "Good luck with the thesis."

Abby fast walks out of the door and closes it softly behind her.

'You need to pull yourself together,' Ralph hears Hiram's voice say in his head. 'If you don't have your wits about you, you'll get us all killed.'

Zack falls into a fitful sleep. The entire time, he dreams that he is stranded at the Halifax ferry station while Abby is out on the Island. He panicked. He has no money and no way to get over to the Island. His fear of losing Abby becomes overwhelming. Zack is startled awake. It takes him a moment to realize where he is. Sleeping around has begun to mess up Zack's bearings. He looks at Abby's alarm clock which says 9:57. He knows that he needs to get a shower but despite that need, he goes to his backpack and pulls his tablet out of his jacket.

Over the next hour, Zack forms the thoughts into this song:

last ferry from Halifax *102 BPM in key of E Major in 4/4 time*

moon riding high above the tide
regrets become my guide
I've missed the last ferry from Halifax
anxiety gives way to panic attack
she's not going to listen to another excuse
she'll just shake her head and cut me loose

gone, gone all gone
not one trinket left to pawn
they'll be no more ferries before dawn
or anyone left I can count upon

last ferry from Halifax
how'd everything get this far off-track
not sure when another is due back
too late for apologies, too soon for a flashback

gone, gone all gone
not one trinket left to pawn
they'll be no more ferries before dawn
or anyone left I can count upon

why didn't I rush before it was too late
my life's gone crooked when it should be straight
she's not going to want to hear anymore
this will be the final slamming of her door

last ferry from Halifax
how'd I get this far off-track
not sure when another is due back
too late for apologies, too soon for a flashback

gone, gone all gone
not one trinket left to pawn
they'll be no more ferries before dawn
or anyone left I can count upon

moon riding high above the tide
regret now my guide

I've missed the last ferry from Halifax
anxiety gives way to panic attack
she's not going to listen to another excuse
she'll shake her head and cut me loose

anxiety gives way to panic attack
I've missed the last ferry from Halifax
why didn't I rush before it got too late
my life's gone crooked when it should be straight

gone, gone all gone
not one trinket left to pawn
they'll be no more ferries before dawn
or anyone left I can count upon

moon riding high above the tide
I've missed the last ferry from Halifax
regrets become my guide
anxiety gives way to panic attack
she's not going to listen to another excuse
she'll shake her head and cut me loose

last ferry from Halifax
how'd I get this far off-track
my life's gone crooked when it should be straight
why didn't I rush before it got too late
not sure when another is due back
too late for apologies, too much too unpack "

Opening boxes

Friday, May 2, 3:26PM. Zack is inside the second large closet inside of the Villa's master bedroom. Zack is putting away the clothes which Abby had a moving company bring over from his trailer on Thursday afternoon. Zack was still unclear how Abby had arranged to get a moving company to operate on such short notice. Abby was in the garage going through the boxes of Zack's clothes and setting aside things which she felt Zack should toss out. So far, the pile of clothing to be tossed out is three times larger than the clothes to be kept.

"RJ, what the hell is this?" hears Abby shouting at him in outrage.

Zack turns to see Abby facing him, her eyes flashing with anger. Zack had seen Abby angry a few times in the past. Zack had never seen Abby this angry. She is holding the printed messages which Zack had pulled from his trailer. Abby's anger has stunned paralyzed Zack.

"Ralph Jones, I need an answer!"

Zack walks to her and as gently as possible guides her out of the closet and to the bed. He sits down beside her. "I found the first sets of messages on the trailer the Wednesday before last," Zack says. "I didn't think much of it. I seemed kind of silly. That "Final Notice" one came the past Wednesday."

"Are these messages why you have the black eye?" Abby asks angrily.

"They are why I have the black eye." Zack says resignedly.

"Did you contact the Island Constabulary?" Abby asks.

"No," Zack replies, "the guy, who gave me this black eye sucker punched me. I made him pay for it."

Abby puts her head into her hands. She begins to say something to Zack but can't form the words. She starts sobbing. Zack slides close to her and puts his left arm around her. She pulls away and rises from the bed. "Who did this?" Abby asks.

"I know who did it," Zack replies. "Some guy from Halifax named Michael Papadopoulos."

Abby snorts in anger.

"I mean who had it done?"

Zack hesitates for a full thirty seconds before responding, "I would guess either your ex-fiancée or your father."

Abby stomps from the room as Zack remains seated upon the bed wondering what's coming next.

Zack hears Clint's voice in his head saying, 'There's smoke over that rise kid. That can't be good."

After a few minutes of silence, Zack can hear Abby shouting into her phone at someone in the next bedroom. The shouting goes on for a full five minutes. Then her voice becomes softer. It's ten more minutes before she comes back into the bedroom.

"It's not my father," Abby says, "but my father is going to get to the bottom of it."

Zack isn't sure if that's good or bad. Zack had only met Abby's father a few times when he was a teenager. He had not exchanged more than ten words with him. Abby's father had seemed aloof and totally disinterested in talking to him. Zack begins to hope that Abby's father getting to the bottom of it, isn't going to involve his own demise.

"You are going to have a bodyguard starting tonight," Abby informs him.

'Christ, kid,' Zack hears Clint's voice say to him. 'You've got to learn to watch your flank. Jihadis aren't going to come up to you and introduce themselves."

Abby walks in front of Zack, who is still seated on the bed. She looks directly into his eyes.

"Why didn't you tell me about these threats?"

"I didn't think they were all that serious," Zack replies.

"We aren't school kids anymore," Abby says. "You are no longer a normal person. I've never been a normal person. You can't take care of this by being the tough guy in the schoolyard and telling the guy, who just told you to stay away from his girl, to "Shove it"."

Familiar Sound

Monday, May 5, 3:46PM. Zack is back on the Island at the Villa preparing to go over to 'The Place' to work with his father, Abe and Beth, on laying out plans for recording of Abe's verses. Zack had dropped Abby off at the university for her trip to Germany yesterday at 3PM. He'd then anxiously ridden back to Wannasea with the bodyguard, who had magically appeared outside of Abby's shared house on Sunday morning.

Riding back to the Island with the bodyguard had been much like making a tour of the city of Fallujah in his Iraq days. Zack had insisted on sitting up front in the vehicle which the bodyguard had told him would be his means of transportation for the foreseeable future. Zack sat beside the driver to watch his every movement. At any moment, he expected the bodyguard to attack him. After arriving at the Villa without incident, Zack had spent most of last night sleepless, pacing the main bedroom. Zack did an hour of his exercises inside his mostly empty closet. At 11AM, when Zack had finally decided to come out of the bedroom, he discovered that he now had a different bodyguard than the one which had driven him to the Island.

'You can't be too cautious in this business,' he'd heard Hiram's voice saying to him most of last night and all this morning.

After a dip in the pool, a long shower and a couple hours reviewing the melodies he was going to present at this afternoon's meeting at 'The Place', the fact that there is now a different person guarding him made Zack feel slightly less anxious.

"Would you mind driving me over to 'The Place'?" Zack asks the new bodyguard, who is standing at the kitchen counter. "I've got some work which I need to do over there."

This bodyguard is somewhat younger than the one Zack drove over from Coventry with yesterday. He was, however, the same size. That size was big.

"Sure,' the man says, "but where's 'The Place'?"

"It's a coffeehouse on the road up to Casino," Zack replies.

The bodyguard pulls out his cell phone and begins tapping on it.

"111 Mountain Way?" the bodyguard asks Zack.

"That's it," Zack says now convinced this particular bodyguard is not from Wannasea Island. "Go ahead and finish your coffee."

Zack sits down on a stool at the kitchen counter facing the man.

"I really liked that song you put out last month," the bodyguard says.

"Which one?" Zack asks.

"Hard Slog," the bodyguard says. "It reminded me of being in Basra."

"You did Iraq?" Zack queries.

"More like Iraq did me," the bodyguard replies, "but I think you know how that works."

"What'd you do there?"

"Pretty much anything the higher ups told me to do," the man replies. "I was a Marine in the 3 Commando Brigade."

"You're one of the dudes, who opened Umm Qasr," Zack comments.

"Me, 7,000 thousand other Booties and a bunch of Yanks," the bodyguard says finishing his coffee and setting his cup in the sink. "Seems odd not being there some days."

"Tell me about it," Zack says with a sigh.

"Let's move out," the bodyguard says.

Zack throws his backpack over his shoulder and walks behind the two-inch taller, thirty-pound heavier ex-Marine to the garage. Zack notices that the car is a slightly different model than the one which he ridden last night.

"Mind if I ride up front with you?" Zack asks. "I'm not used to this being chauffeured nonsense."

"Knock yourself out," the bodyguard tells him.

Zack throws his backpack and acoustic guitar onto the rear seat before opening the front door and climbing onto the passenger side.

"You spent most of your time in 'the Big Suck' up North," the ex-Marine says to Zack, "didn't you?"

"We started out down by Basra when I first got there in '08," Zack replies. "We moved up to Anbar in February of '09."

"How are you linked up with Halifax Shipbuilding?" the ex-Marine asks.

"Do you know who Abby Phillips is?" Zack asks.

"Never heard of her," the bodyguard replies, "but there is some guy named Phillips who runs the company."

"Abby is his daughter," Zack says.

"And you are her...?" the ex-Marine says leaving his question unfinished.

"Boyfriend for lack of a better term," Zack replies as the car moves out of the complex and on to South Mountain Way.

"Must be pretty serious boyfriend to warrant this treatment," the bodyguard says.

"Abby and I have a history," Zack replies.

The ex-Marine goes silent as he follows his cellphone's direction to 'The Place'.

As they pass the roundabout and head toward the entrance to 'The Place', Zack sees sixteen New Jericho protestors lining the road across from the entrance. The protestors are carrying signs which read:

"Your End is Nigh"

"Repent while you are able."

"God's Judgement is coming, and the Prophet Ainsley will lead it"

"Free the Prophet. Restore God's Dominion".

Zack hears the man at the head of the protestors calling out through a bullhorn, "Free the Prophet. Prepare for judgement, ye spawns of Satan".

"Interesting lot," the bodyguard says. "Are they your welcoming committee?"

"I don't think so," Zack replies. "You can park anywhere. The coffeehouse isn't open today. We are just using the place to plan some recording sessions."

There are only two other cars in the parking lot. Zack's VW which is parked at the far west end toward the patio and a service vehicle. The ex-Marine parks the car in the front row, two spots left of the main entrance.

Zack swings out of the passenger side of the vehicle and pulls his things out of the back seat. The bodyguard comes over beside him.

"You don't need to come in if you don't want to," Zack tells him.

"Sorry," the bodyguard says, "my job is to keep you in my sights at all times when you are off Phillip's property."

The front door of 'The Place' is unlocked. Zack sees a spread of goodies as well as tea and coffee lined up next to Abe's normal table where Molly, Beth and Abe are currently sitting.

The ex-Marine goes to the table nearest the front door and sits down before saying, "Not being anti-social but no introductions please. Just treat me like part of the furniture."

Zack gives the bodyguard a chagrined smile and walks over to where Abe and Beth are sitting.

"Who's your friend?" Abe asks.

"I now have a full-time bodyguard," Zack replies. "I've been instructed that we are to treat him as if he is part of the furniture."

"Was the bodyguard your idea?" Abe asks as Zack pulls his tablet and a manila folder from his backpack.

"No," Zack replies, "he's a gift from Abby's father."

Abe raises his eyebrows. Zack notices that Molly has scowled when he said "Abby's father".

"I'm glad to see your eye is doing better," Beth says.

Zack decides that it is not in his best interest to say that his eye is doing better as the result of Abby's treating it.

"Is Dave going to be doing any recording today?" Molly asks.

"No," Zack replies, "Dave won't be here today. Today is going to be just a planning session for the background music and to begin working on the sequence of recording."

Normally Molly would have been over today's plan three times by now and produced a printed agenda. Zack knew that there was now a large space between him, Molly and what used to be normal.

"Would you tell him that he owes me billing for your last two session when you see him?" Molly asks.

"Sure," Zack replies, "I'm planning on being over at the studio most of tomorrow."

"Mind if I see if your bodyguard wants something to drink or eat?" Molly asks.

"Not at all," Zack says. "He seems to be a nice enough guy, but I'll warn you that he takes his job very seriously."

"So do I," Molly says with more than a little bite in her words.

Molly rises from her chair and goes over to the ex-Marine. She stands talking to him as Abe describes to Beth and Zack, the verses he thinks should be included. After getting a cup of coffee for Zack's bodyguard, Molly returns to the table and begins taking notes and making a planning schedule. For the next hour they continue in this manner until Zack's father comes in with his fiddle. After small talk, Beth, Zack, and his father begin playing various melodies for the verses. Abe listens and provides his opinion.

A little after 6:30, Molly stops her note taking and asks, "Is anyone else here hungry?"

Zack, who has not eaten anything since a late lunch with Abby yesterday, say, "Now that you mention it, I'm famished?"

"How about if I order some Chinese?" Molly asks.

"Sounds good to me," Beth says.

After getting Abe's and Hank's agreement, Molly walks behind the bar and picks up a notepad and pencil. She carries them to the table. Molly then brings up the menu for 'Duck & Dumplings' restaurant which is located near Wannasea Extension on to her tablet. In turn Molly goes to everyone, including the bodyguard, and gets their selection. When complete, she phones the order in.

Beth, Hank, and Zack are at the piano, when Molly walks up and asks Zack, "Can you give me the keys for your Bug. We are too far out for them deliver, so I'm going to need to go pick up our order."

Zack goes into his backpack behind the chair at Abe's table and pulls his keys out from the front pocket.

"I think there should be enough gas in it," Zack says. " I haven't driven it much lately."

"We've noticed," Molly says as she takes Zacks keys and walks across the dining room then out the front door.

Zack is back at the piano beside Beth when he hears a tremendous "WOMPH" coming from outside, followed by the sound of debris hitting the front of 'The Place". The cups and saucers under the counter rattle loudly.

Zack knows this sound all too well. It is the sound which haunts his dreams. It is the sound which sent him flying that fateful day in Hit.

Almost by instinct Zack is across the floor and headed out the front door. The ex-Marine is two steps in front of him carrying a fire extinguisher which he has pulled down from the front wall.

Flames are shooting three feet above the top of Zack's Volkswagen. What's left of the front half of the car is a mangled mess. Nothing can be seen of Molly. The ex-Marine with Zack at his heels, runs as close to the burning vehicle as possible and begins spraying the car with the fire extinguisher. Zack starts trying to move toward the driver's door but is pulled back by the bodyguard, who begins backing Zack toward the entrance to 'The Place'.

"Don't go any closer," the ex-Marine instructs Beth, Abe and Hank, "there's nothing we can do for her anymore. If that gas tank goes, there will just be more casualties."

"I've called Emergency Services," Beth says in a shaking voice. "They'll be here any moment."

The sound of sirens can be heard coming up from the village.

Zack can't force his eyes off the burning wreckage.

"I expected this in Iraq," Zack thinks aloud, "I wasn't expecting it here."

"None of us were," the ex-Marine says.

Rage begins to fill Zack's being.

"I'm going to find whoever is responsible for this and kill them with my bare hands!" Zack suddenly screams out. "Molly didn't deserve anything like this. What the hell did she ever do to hurt anyone?"

"No, she didn't deserve this," Zack's father comes up beside Zack and puts his arm around his son, "but raging about isn't going to help right now."

"I'm not raging, Dad," Zack says angrily. "I am making a commitment. I will find out who did this. I will kill them."

A fire engine and ambulance sped on to the property. By the time that engine had been connected to the fire hydrant as the west corner of the driveway and begun to spray Zack's smoldering Volkswagen, three squad cars pull up. Jack Druce jumps out of the first vehicle and goes immediately to the small crowd in front of 'The Place'.

"Let's go inside folks," Druce instructs. "There really isn't anything we can do to help out here but get in the way."

The lieutenant leads Beth, Abe, Hank, Zack, and his bodyguard inside. He guides them to the front tables by the stage and asks them to sit. A young sergeant follows them inside.

"I will need to interview you individually," Druce says. "Let's start with you."

The lieutenant is pointing to the ex-Marine.

Druce, the sergeant, and bodyguard walk to the table in the farthest reach of the dining area.

Abe returns to talking to Defense One on his cell phone. Beth, Zack, and Hank sit in shocked silence, both trying to comprehend what has transpired.

After five minutes, Druce returns to the table. The bodyguard leaves with the sergeant through the front door.

"Mr. Jones, your turn next,' Druce instructs.

The interview with Zack's father takes less time. When Hank is finished, he is led out the front door.

Druce spends almost ten minutes talking with Beth before coming to the table and asking for Abe.

After Abe has left the table, Zack notices that Abe has left his open cell phone behind on the table. Zack sees that there are three new messages in Abe's inbox from Defense One.

Zack picks up Abe's phone and opens the latest message. He glances at the attached video recordings. He forwards that message as well as the two which proceeded it to his own email address. Zack then closes all messages and uses the 'File' tab to mark all 3 as unread. A few more minutes pass before Druce comes to the table and sits down across from Zack.

"What the hell is going on Ralph?" Druce asks. "Why the bodyguard? Why your car?"

Zack starts with Abby dumping her fiancée and goes through the whole story up to Druce's arrival. The only thing Zack leaves out is the choking and tie-wrapping of Michael Papadopoulos.

"Why didn't you come to us?" Druce asks.

Zack shrugs his shoulders, then says, "I didn't think it was that serious. Those printed messages seemed like something a school kid might make."

"Still think that?" Druce asks.

"No," Zack says with a grimace.

"Grab your stuff," Druce instructs. "You're coming with me."

"Where are we going?" Zack asks.

"I'm taking you into custody," Druce says firmly.

Zack is stunned. It takes him a minute to process what Druce is saying.

"You suspect me of killing Molly?" Zack asks with an increasing feeling of hopelessness.

"No, I don't suspect you or anything other than burning with desire for revenge," Druce replies. "I want you where we can keep an eye on you to make certain that nobody else gets hurt."

Exit Stage Left

Wednesday, May 7, 9:41PM. Zack is on-stage at 'The Shell' working through his last set. The Constabulary had thought it a good idea to have Zack do his scheduled performance in hopes of drawing out the two individuals, who they had on video planting the bomb in Zack's VW. Their hopes lie in Defense One and their own surveillance efforts. There were now plain-clothed law enforcement everywhere around 'the Place'. Phil, a member of the Constabulary, is monitoring Zack from the backstage wing.

Zack had spent the past 48 hours housed in the holding cell at the Constabulary. The officers were very loose about his custody. Zack was allowed to use all the devices in his backpack and given access to the station's wi-fi. He was allowed out of his cell whenever he wanted. Last evening, when he saw the duty officers playing pinochle in their holding area, he even sat in for three hands after one of the officers had been called to handle a domestic dispute. Zack had learned to play pinochle from Hiram. Other than that, Zack had spent most of the time either speaking with Abby or on his tablet working through the videos which he'd forwarded from Abe's cell phone. Zack had developed four very good images of the individuals who had placed the bomb in Zack's VW early last Saturday morning. His car had sat armed with the bomb which killed Molly for over two days. Sitting in the holding cell had also given Zack plenty of opportunity to dwell on the fact that Molly's death had come from a bomb which had been placed in his vehicle for the express purpose of killing him, not Molly. Once again, the survivor's guilt has begun to overwhelm Zack. The only thing holding Zack back from it, is his burning desire to avenge Molly's death.

Over the past two days, Zack had been facetiming Abby almost as much as he had been able to work on the security videos and plotting how to begin tracking down Molly's killers. Dealing with Abby had been something else.

Abby had not gotten the news of the explosion and Zack being in custody until yesterday afternoon. Much of their time since had been spent talking about Molly. After much prodding from Abby, Zack had disclosed to her how guilty, sad, and confused, he was feeling over Molly's death. Abby has tried to convince Zack that she is more responsible for Molly's death than he probably is. Abby promises that she will do everything in her power to help Zack not only bring Molly's killers to justice but find a fitting way to pay tribute to Molly's legacy and make certain that the Island will not forget her.

Abby's next reaction had been to attempt to arrange to fly back from Germany. It had taken three thirty-minute sessions and having a discussion with Jack Druce to convince Abby to remain with her group. Druce explained that the Constabulary was not going to allow her in to see Zack for more than 30 minutes a day. Abby had not liked it, but she'd finally accepted that she could see more of Zack using FaceTime than she would if she were to come to Wannasea.

This had been one of Zack's most lethargic performances. He can't get visions of Molly out of his mind. At the start of the second set, Zack had told the audience to hang on to their tickets to be used at a replacement session sometime next month. Three times during the first session, he had referenced Molly's death and apologized for his performance.

Zack's eyes constantly shift to the wing of the stage area, where Phil, the officer currently assigned to watch him, is standing. As Zack plays the third song of his second set, he's come up with a plan. Seeing Phil move into the shadows, Zack knows that the officer is now moving out of the backstage area to switch off with one of his counterparts.

Zack turns to his father and whispers, "You guys close out the next two songs. I've got to go hit the head."

Without waiting for his father to answer, Zack sets down his guitar and fast walks into the backstage area. He grabs his windbreaker off the hook on the wall. As fast as Zack is able, he moves out the side backstage door.

On a run, Zack jumps on the hood of 'The Place's' Vauxhall delivery van which is parked beside the fence on the side leading to woods running up to the old Government Center. Zack propels himself on top of the van's roof, then uses it to go over the fence. He hits the ground like a cat and does not stop running through the surrounding woods until he has reached the back area of Mountain Village. Slowing to a fast walk, Zack goes directly to Mollie's unit. He is surprised to see that it is not secured by police tape. As the lights on the deck switch on, Zack goes to the front door and enters the last six digits of Molly's cellphone number to unlock it. Zack goes inside without turning on the lights and moves past the kitchen area to the dressing closet where Molly keeps her clothes. He switches on the small overhead light. Zack fishes through the bottom drawer and pulls out a long brunette wig which Molly would wear when she was in a hurry. He tears off his windbreaker and shirt and begins looking through Mollie's clothes. Molly is much smaller than Zack, so he selects a flowered mu-mu which Molly had used as a dressing gown. Zack pulls it over his head tearing the back a little as it settles on his frame. The dress had come to Mollies mid-calf. It barely reaches Zack's knees. However, with his jeans still on, it looks acceptable. Zack positions the wig on his head using two clips to clasp it to his own hair. Zack looks in the mirror. If someone looks closely, he's not going to fool them. Particularly with his deck shoes still on. Zack picks up his windbreaker which contains his cellphone, then quickly goes into the kitchen. He opens the right drawer where he knows Molly keeps the key to her Vespa. Along with the Vespa key, he finds a stash of bills.

"I owe you, Molly," Zack says as he takes the bills and shoves them into his jeans pocket. Putting his windbreaker back on, he pulls the hood up over his head and goes out of Molly's unit to the small patio where the Vespa is chained around the front post which holds up the awning. Zack enters the last four digits of Molly's phone and the lock pops open. Zack stuffs the lock into the pocket of his windbreaker. He turns on the engine and drives the scooter off the deck, onto the path past the shared facilities and out to the Mountain Village exit to Mountain Way. Zack swings left and guides the scooter toward the Village.

Once at the ferry dock, Zack secures Molly's scooter to one the posts allocated for two-wheel vehicles to the left of the ferry's entrance. The ferry is just pulling into the pier. Zack remains standing beside Molly's scooter for a good five minutes until the ferry crew begins allowing passengers to enter. Zack pays for his fare out of the bills in his pocket rather than using his toll card. He sticks to the shadow side of the walkway and the ferry and finds a spot up front near the dinghies. He positions himself between two of the dinghies and leans his back against the starboard side of the ferry. He pulls out his cellphone and enters a message to Abby, "Sorry but I have to do this. Please, please don't worry. I will do everything in my power to be there to pick you up on Sunday. I love you Abigail. Please remain in Germany until your performances have finished. Please don't give up on me." Zack hits send, then pulls the back off his cell phone and removes his SIM card. He places it in his wallet. He knows that in about forty minutes Abby is going to start becoming frantic when she cannot contact him.

As the ferry pulls away from the pier, Zack fishes in his jean pocket for the money which he has pulled from Molly's drawer.

He counts $455. Adding the $5 he had used for his fare; Zack now owes Molly $460 in addition to his other now unpayable debts to her. With the money in his own wallet, Zack has almost $800 in cash. He hopes that will be enough to help him track down Michael Papadopoulos.

Zack completes the ferry trip to Halifax between the two dinghies. As he thinks of Molly, his rage grows. This is followed by thoughts of Abby and the hope that what he has done is not going to freak her out so badly that she is going to cut him loose.

Zack waits until most of the few passengers on the upper deck have made their way down the gangplank. With his head down, he walks crisply behind them, still trying to stick to the shadows as he exits the ferry. Zack fast walks to the first taxi in line across from the Halifax ferry station.

"Jewel's" Zack says to the cab driver.

When the taxi has gone the short distance to the bar, Zack asks him to drive around back. He hands the driver a $20 for the $7 fare and tells him to keep the change. Zack waits until the cab has left before turning and quickly walking the three blocks to Alfie's apartment. He glances at his watch. 11:22. Zack climbs the stairs to the apartment and sits on the final step. He is there for over an hour before he hears Alfie, Cheri and the Donna Summer impersonator walking toward him. They stop after spotting Zack seated on their steps.

"Hello," Cheri Pie calls out, "do we know you?"

"It's me," Zack calls back to him.

Alfie comes up the stairs with Cheri Pie close at her heels.

"Zack," Alfie says, "what are you doing here and why are you dressed like this?"

"You really are going to have to work on your look honey, if you are coming over to our side," Cheri Pie says.

Zack laughs despite himself.

"Can we go inside and talk?" Zack asks.

The pair lead him into the kitchen with Donna Summer's impersonator following them.

Zack takes five minutes to explain what he has done.

"Are you willing to let me hide out here, tonight?" Zack asks. "It will not be without possible legal complications, but I swear to you whatever happens, I'll not only help you get out of it but make it right with you."

"We aren't all that enamored of the law around here," Cheri Pie says. "I'm game to help Zack out, what about you girls?"

Alfie and the other lady nod their agreement.

"You can share my room if you'd like," Cheri Pie says with a wiggle and a wink. "I'll do your couch if it's okay," Zack replies.

Alfie leads Zack into the living room and sits him down on the couch.

"Why are you over here?" Alfie asks.

Zack explains about Michael Papadopoulos and that his plan is to track him down tomorrow in the hope that he will identify the individuals who put the explosives in his VW.

"Honey," Donna Summer's lookalike says, "you shouldn't be messing around with people like that. That's a job for the police."

"You don't know this dude," Alfie says rather defensively. "Zack's probably better at taking care of himself than any of the cops around here are."

"He doesn't look like a badass," Cheri Pie says. "He looks like a sweetie."

"Believe me," Alfie says, "Zack is one bad dude."

Path To Nowhere

Thursday, May 8, 8:17AM. Zack is seated at the kitchen table with Cheri Pie drinking coffee. Alfie has just gone off to his guitar lesson after being urged by Zack that the best thing which he can do for him is to act normal.

The Donna Summer impersonator walks in and sits down.

"You are all over the news" she says to Zack. " They think somebody has snatched you."

Zack takes a sip of his coffee.

"How can we help you track down this guy, you are looking for?" Cheri Pie asks.

"To start," Zack asks, "do you think you could help me rent a car? I've got about five hundred on me."

"I can do better than that," Cherry Pie says. "I can lend you, my Citroen."

"I'll pay you back for it," Zack says.

"We'll worry about that later," Cheri Pie says. "What's after a car?"

"I need to go buy a burner phone plus a digital camera, then make some copies," Zack replies. "After that I'm going to the address that I have for Papadopoulos."

"First I think we need to get you dressed properly," Cherry Pie replies. "Whatever this ensemble you have on is called, it doesn't work at any level."

Cheri Pie turns to the Donna Summer impersonator and says, "Babs, can you run down to the Thrift and pick up something in the next size up from yours which says professional lady?"

"Sure thing," Babs says rising from the table.

Zack reaches for his wallet to give Babs money.

"Worry about that later," Babs says pushing Zack's hand back toward his wallet. "I have a running tab down there. I'll be back in about twenty minutes."

"See if they have any size 12 flats, fake glasses and maybe and a decent sized purse," Cheri Pie says to the departing Babs. "I'm going to work on this hair and face."

Cheri Pie rises and goes through the living room. Zack sips coffee until she returns with Molly's wig, which he had taken off last night, and a plastic container full of makeup. Cheri Pie sits on the kitchen table.

"Turn yourself around, sweetie," Cheri Pie says as she goes to the sink and wets a fresh dishcloth with warm water.

Cheri Pie first cleans Zack's face, then uses the dishcloth to wet Zack's hair.

"This really isn't a bad wig,' Cheri Pie says as she picks it up and attaches it properly to Zack's hair.

She walks back into her bedroom and returns with a curling iron and extension cord which is plugged into the outlet on the kitchen wall.

"I think you need to have some curls," Cheri Pie says as she brushes out the wig.

"I used to be a hairdresser before I got into performing,' Cheri Pie says. "Being a hairdresser is a big asset in this business."

Once satisfied with the soft curls at the end of the wig on Zack's head, Cheri Pie turns to doing his face. As she completes his eyebrows, Babs comes back in carrying a pair of flat women's shoes, lavender shirt, Tweed business outfit and a dark brown Mimi bag. Babs pulls a pair of large black rimmed glasses from her purse, drops the shoes on the floor and then sets everything on the table.

Cheri Pie next does the blush and finishes up with a demur shade of wine-colored lipstick.

"Go put that outfit on," Cheri Pie instructs. "Don't worry how it fits. We'll quick trim it."

Zack rises, picks up the tweed suit and goes into the bathroom. When he returns, Babs says, "Not bad but let's trim it a little."

Babs and Cheri Pie set to putting pins in the suit.

"Take it off and I'll sew it," Babs instructs.

Zack pulls off the suit and hands it to Babs and disappears into her bedroom.

"She's a whiz with the Singer," Cheri Pie tells him. "Let's see how that shirt fits."

Zack begins to put it on before Cheri Pie stops him.

"You need to take off that t-shirt," she advises.

Reluctantly Zack pulls off his t-shirt.

Cheri Pie gasps when she sees his back.

"Oh honey, were did that come from?"

"Iraq,' Zack responds hoping the conversation doesn't go further.

Cheri Pie hands him back the lavender shirt and helps him put it on.

"I don't think we have to do anything with the shirt," Cheri Pie advises before she disappears to her bedroom.

Cheri Pie returns with a pair of panty hose.

"Put these on," she says after opening the package.

Zack pulls on the pantyhose. He feels as if he has forced himself into a sausage casing. "You've got some pretty decent legs," Cheri Pie says as Bab returns with the pant suit.

Zack puts on the pant suit then slides into the flats which are only a little too small. Cheri Pie takes the glasses from the table and puts them on Zack.

"Not bad," Babs says. "Not bad at all."

"Let's go see yourself," Cheri Pie says leading Zack to a full-length mirror on the wall beside the refrigerator.

Zack is shocked by the image which comes back at him. He looks like a bigger version of Molly in her business attire. Zack immediately forces the thought from his mind. It brings too much anger and grief.

"I don't know how to thank you," Zack says.

"You don't have to," Babs says. "As long as we don't go to jail, this isa story that we will both be telling our grandkids."

"Let's go get to that other stuff," Cheri Pie says as she pulls a faux silk pink jack down from a hook by the entrance.

Cheri leads Zack to her 1994 champagne colored Citroën XM. Cheri drives to the Office Supply store close to Zack's favorite restaurant for Halibut.

"I'll do the talking," Cheri Pie says. "You just act demur."

First, they make a couple picture quality photos from the Defense One images which Zack has trimmed.

"What are your plans for those pictures?" Cheri Pie whispers to Zack.

"Hopefully I'll discover where Papadopoulos works, and I'll take pictures of everyone coming and going. Then I'll try to match them to these photos."

"I've got an idea," Cheri says. "I've been working around here for over ten years. I know a lot of people. Why don't we make some more copies, and I will pass them out to the people that I trust and have them call me back."

"These are dangerous people, Cheri," Jack cautions.

"I'm a big girl," Cheri replies. "Like you, I've had plenty of practice taking care of myself."

"Why don't we stick Papadopoulos' photo with these photos along with his name?" Zack suggests.

They spend ten minutes adding then trimming the picture which Zack has from Papadopoulos' driver license to the pictures from Defense One. They have forty copies made.

Next, they go to the cellphones and Zack picks out two CityTalk, no contract models. They follow this up by selecting a $150 digital camera. Zack grabs a small stack of manila folders before they head to check out. Zack remains behind Cheri Pie as they go through check out and have the phone activated. Both phones have Cheri's real name of Roger Davis displayed on their screen.

"Why two phones," Cheri asks as they return to her car. "One is for you," Zack replies. "You don't want to be contacting me from your own phone. Use the burner to call me if you get something back from distributing the fliers."

Cheri flips her keys to Zack.

"You drive. I'll plug all the necessary numbers into these phones."

They go back to Cheri's car.

"Where to?" Zack asks.

"Drop me off by Jewel's." Cheri advises, "I can walk around and deliver these photos. You can then go try to track down the guy that you are looking for."

Zack maneuvers the Citroën the three and half miles back to Jewel's as Cheri places the photos in manila folders. Cheri takes the thickest folder and exits the car.

"Take good care of my baby," she says as she exits the car. "I'll call you the minute I hear anything."

Zack drives the car back to Cheri's apartment parking lot. There he plugs the street address from Papadopoulos' driver license into the new cellphone's mapping program. He restarts the car and finds himself backtracking from where he had just been. He ends up in front of an apartment complex about two miles west of the office supply store where he'd made the photos.

Zack spends twenty minutes circling the parking lot and the surrounding streets looking for the silver Ford four door. He finds a few cars which are similar, but none have the right license plate. Noticing the gas is getting low, Zack drives down the street a few miles to the nearest gas station and fills the tank paying in cash. Zack has to use the manual in the glove compartment to figure out how to spring the fuel door.

Zack returns to the apartment complex he came from and parks the car. He spends two hours waiting for Papadopoulos to appear and learning the workings of the digital camera.

At 1:25, his new cell phone which is on the passenger seat rings. Zack quickly reaches over and grabs it.

"I've got a lead on the Papadopoulos guy," Cheri says. "He's a bouncer at a dive called 'Guys and Dolls'. He's supposedly someone not to mess with."

"Thank you, Cheri," Zack says. "If you were here, I'd kiss you."

"Don't make promises you can't keep," Cheri says. "I've heard nothing about the people in the other photos, but I'll call you if I hear anything."

"You are a princess," Zack says.

"Actually, I'm the queen," Cheri replies, "but I'll forgive you. You are still learning."

With that Cheri disconnects the call.

Zack looks up 'Guys and Dolls' on his cellphone then drives a little less than two miles to the place. It is surrounded by an industrial area and a few seedy bars. Zack spots the silver Ford parked three rows back in the Guys and Dolls parking lot. He parks as close to the vehicle as he can get and suppresses the urge to go inside and confront Papadopoulos.

Zack uses the cell phone to look up the number for 'Guys and Dolls'. He dials the number. A female voice answers.

"Is Michael Papadopoulos there?" Zack asks.

"You mean Mike?" comes back to him.

"Yeah, Mike Papadopoulos," Zack says. "Sorry."

"Who should I say is calling?" the lady asks.

'Good question,' Zack thinks before responding, "Ralph".

A few seconds pass before the lady comes back on the line, "Mike says he don't know no Ralph."

"Tell him it's Ralph from out on Wannasea Island," Zack replies. "We met about a week ago. I really need to talk with him about some mutual business."

The lady puts the phone down. The line is silent for almost two minutes before a gruff voice comes on the phone, "What hell are you doing calling me? We are through with you. We don't have no more business to discuss."

"I think we do," Zack replies.

"Talk costs money, kid," Papadopoulos replies. "My time comes at a price."

"I've got about $400," Zack replies. "How much talk will that buy me?"

"Maybe 10 minutes. Depends on my mood. Why don't you come here, and we'll talk."

"I'd prefer not to," Zack replies. "Why don't you come out to the parking lot? I'm parked in a gold-colored Citroën."

Papadopoulos seems to think about it for a minute before saying, "You'd better have the $400 dollars with you. If there are any cops around, you'll be a dead man."

"I think you know that I'm avoiding cops at the moment," Zack replies.

"Yeah," Papadopoulos replies, "that's what I've heard. Citroën you say?"

"I'm parked a row behind you," Zack replies.

The phone is disconnected. Papadopoulos comes out the entrance of 'Guys and Dolls". He is followed by two slightly larger, younger men. Papadopoulos motions for them to remain at the entrance as he walks to the Citroën. Zack has cleared off the passenger seat. He has the folder with the photos in it on his lap. He's placed the digital camera in the glove compartment. Zack swings the passenger door open.

"What the hell!" Papadopoulos says as he sees Zack. "Is this how you usually dress?"

"It is when I'm trying to avoid the law," Zack replies.

Papadopoulos gives him a weird smile and climbs into the passenger seat.

"Open your shirt," Papadopoulos instructs Zack.

Zack unbuttons the shirt and Papadopoulos pats him down then follows it up by feeling under the dash for microphones. Finding none, he opens the glovebox and pulls out the digital camera.

"Whose is this," Papadopoulos asks.

"Don't have a clue," Zack lies. "This is not my car."

Papadopoulos fiddles with the camera for a few minutes before turning it off, removing its batteries and shoving it back into the glove compartment.

"Where's the money?" Papadopoulos asks.

Zack pulls the $400 out of the left pant suit jacket pocket and hands it to Papadopoulos.

"What do you want to talk about?"

Zack opens the manila folder and hands the photos to Papadopoulos.

"Do you know either of these two people?" Zack asks.

Papadopoulos looks carefully at the pictures, before saying, "You're the fourth person this week who has asked me about these mooks. I wouldn't tell the other three if I did know those people. Based on circumstances, I'll tell you honestly that I've never seen either of those two and I know most of the people around here who are in my line of work."

Zack frowns and takes back the photos.

"Let me clue you in," Papadopoulos says, "after our little meeting over on your island, my boss got rather pissed at the stuffed shirt, who hired us to scare you off. That person not only lied about you messing around with somebody else's wife, they lied about who you were. We thought we were dealing with some Ralph guy living in a trailer out on the Island. We not only washed our hands of the whole thing, we passed along your message to him and added a little message of our own. We told them that if they came after you again, we'd join with you and take them apart piece by little piece. We have our standards. We don't go in for BS like that."

Zack notices that the two guys at the entrance are now coming toward the car. Papadopoulos tries to roll his window down.

"How does this damned thing work?" Papadopoulos asks.

"This really isn't my car," Zack says. "I don't know." Papadopoulos opens the door and takes a step out of the car. He motions for the two men to go back.

"We're good here," Papadopoulos calls to the men.

They turn around and don't stop walking until they've gone back into 'Guys and Dolls'.

Papadopoulos sits back down in the passenger seat leaving the door slightly ajar.

"You've still got time on the clock, kid."

"What where those printed messages on my trailer's windows about it?" Zack asks, unable to really think of anything else.

Papadopoulos laughs.

"We tried for over a week to call your cell phone," Papadopoulos says. "Despite every damned thing we tried, all we were able to do was get to your answering service. We don't leave threats in voice mail or with answering services. My English ain't the best. When I had trouble finding you and getting your attention, printing out those messages was the next best thing that I could come up with."

"When you posted that first set of messages," Zack asks, "how long had you been trying to get in touch with me?"

Papadopoulos thinks for a moment, "We were hired to deal with you on the 4th of April, so a little over a week."

This date surprises Zack. It is almost two weeks before Abby came to his trailer's door.

"Have you heard anything more about the client who hired you to come after me or if he's hired someone else?"

"I've heard," Papadopoulos replies, "that client got squeezed. Less than a week ago, he started getting serious pressure to stop trying to get to you. He was threatened with being outed to the Press. Seems he's in a position that the Press can do him real harm. We also heard his old man got so pissed at him that he's shipped his ass off to Estonia for the next month."

This news really doesn't make Zack feel any better or any safer.

"Listen kid," Papadopoulos says. "I'm going to give you some free professional advice. I've been in this business going on thirty years. We don't come after anyone that don't owe someone something. When we come after someone and the desired outcome is that they disappear, it's a shot to the back of the head, then a swim with the fishes after a long boat ride and being cut into bait. That's how things work with us."

Zack absorbs the information trying to decide where that leaves him.

"Blowing up cars and people is for amateurs or loonies with some kind of crazy axe to grind. Those kinds of people don't just want you to disappear. Those kinds of people are hellbent on making your disappearance a statement. That car of yours blowing up with the girl in it, is that kind of statement. I'm pretty sure that you are fishing in the wrong pond."

"This isn't the way that I expected our talk to go," Zack says.

"But that's the way things are," Papadopoulos says. "All you can do is accept it and move on. That wasn't your girlfriend in that car, was it?"

"No," Zack says very hesitantly, "it was my best friend."

"You've got a helluva complicated life, kid," Papadopoulos comments.

"You're the second person in a week, who has told me that," Zack replies.

Papadopoulos pulls open the car door, "We're done here. I really hope you find what you are looking for kid. Have a good life."

Papadopoulos climbs out of the car. Closes the door and walks directly back into 'Guys and Dolls'.

'You've really screwed the pooch on this one, kid,' Zack hears Clint's voice saying in his head.

Zack knows that he has not only let Molly down. He's let his family down. He's endangered Alfie and his roommates for no good reason. He's let Abby down. He's muddled things up. Muddled them up just about as badly as he can.

Downcast, Zack starts up the Citroën and drives directly back to Alfie's apartment. He pulls all his folders and pictures out of the car. He leaves the digital camera in the Citroën's glovebox. Zacks' climbs the stairs and knocks on the door of Alfie's apartment. Alfie lets him in.

"You don't look like things went well," Alfie says.

"No, they didn't," Zack replies. "I've discovered that I've been fishing in the wrong pond as Mike Papadopoulos says." Bab's, who is sitting at the table says, "Welcome to our world. We are always fishing in the wrong pond."

"Let me get you a cup of coffee," Alfie says.

Zack plops the folders in the middle of the table. He's losing energy by the nano-second. Cheri Pie comes into the room and sits down.

"No luck with that Papadopoulos guy I take it?" Cheri says.

"Worse than no luck," Zack says. "I really want to apologize to the three of you. When I came here last night, I really believed that I was on the path to avenge Molly's killing. What I've done is put you at risk and succeeded in making a damned fool of myself."

"What are you going to do?" Cheri asks.

Alfie, who had just walked in from his guitar lesson with Earl Evans before Zack knocked, carries a steaming cup of coffee to the table. He sets it down in front of Zack then takes an empty chair. Both Alfie and Babs begin leafing through the photos inside the folders which Zack has placed on the table.

"I'm going to go back to the island and give myself up," Zack replies. "Then I'm going to start apologizing to anyone who is willing to listen to me. I've managed to make things worse."

This is as deflated as Zack felt after Hit. He has no one to blame but himself.

"I know these guys," Alfie suddenly blurts out holding out the photographs from Zack's folder.

"What do you mean?" Zack asks.

"I know these two guys," Alfie says firmly.

"This is Elmer Ainsley," Alfie says holding out the picture of the older of the two men. "He's the Prophet's cousin."

"This is Stanley," Alfie says holding out the photo of the second individual identified by Defense One surveillance. "I'm not sure of his last name but he's the Prophet's nephew."

"You are absolutely certain?" Zack asks incredulously.

"Would you forget people, who made your life miserable for over a year," Alfie replies in a hurt tone. "Those two tried to shove a banana up my bum at a church mixer."

Zack weighs his options. He pulls the burner phone out of his purse. He goes to the Wannasea Constabulary website and selects the phone number for their service desk. The call rings twice before being answered by the desk sergeant.

"This is Ralph Jones," Zack says, "I need to speak with Lieutenant Druce."

The desk sergeant seems reluctant to believe that it is actually Zack on the phone.

"I left my backpack and tablet in the holding cell," Zack says. "Now please let me speak to Jack Druce."

Zack hears a bunch of shouting and rustling of paper. It takes 90 seconds before Jack Druce comes to the phone.

"Where are you, Ralph?" Druce asks.

"I'm going to be heading back to the Island," Zack says, "but before we get into that, you need to know that the two individuals, who Defense One captured on video putting the explosive in my car, are Edgar Ainsley's cousin and nephew."

"You are sure of this?" Druce asks.

Alfie nods his head before Zack says to Druce, "The cousin's name is Elmer Ainsley. The nephew's first name is Stanley but I'm not certain about his last name."

"I'm going to turn you over to Phil," Druce says to Zack. "He'll make arrangements to pick you up."

Zack hears more commotion before Phil comes on the phone.

"I thought you liked us better than to give us the slip, Zack,' Phil tells Zack.

"I apologize," Zack replies.

"When will you be at the ferry station?" Phil asks.

"As soon as I can get myself collected and catch the ferry," Zack replies.

"We could come get you," Phil replies.

"I think, it's better if I come to you," Zack counters. "You'll understand when I get there."

"We'll be at the ferry exit," Phil replies.

Zack disconnects the call, rises from his chair, and begins collecting his jacket.

"Let's spruce you up a little before you head out," Cheri says using her kit to touch Zack up. "I'll drive you to the ferry."

Zack takes his cellphone from his windbreaker pocket and places it into the purse.

"I don't know how to thank you," Zack says as soon as he's pulled himself together. "If there's anything which I owe you for or anything you need, all you have to do is call."

"Don't you want me to come over with you and verify the pictures?" Alfie says.

"Let's leave you out of this if we can," Zack says leaning into Alfie and giving her a hug.

Zack walks to Babs and hugs her before following Cheri down to the Citroën.

It takes less than three minutes for Cheri to get to the ferry station.

"I can't begin to thank you," Zack replies. "Let me know if there is anything at all that I can do for you."

"Just come back and see us," Cheri says with a laugh before driving off. "Things are exciting when you are around."

Zack doesn't bother sticking to the shadows as he walks on to the waiting ferry. He walks up to the front benches and takes a seat before pulling his cellphone and wallet out of his purse. Zack takes the SIM card out, opens the back of phone and carefully inserts the chip. His phone begins buzzing like crazy a minute after he has turned it on. The list of phone calls and messages from Abby is long and daunting. Zack tries calling her number but is dumped into voice mail.

"Hi Abby," Zack says, "this is Zack. I'm headed back to the island. The Constabulary knows I'm coming. I'm fine. I'm sorry if I've worried you and hope you will forgive me. I love you so much I can hardly stand it."

Zack disconnects the call and then sends her a message saying essentially the same thing.

Next Zack calls his mother, who answers on the second ring. "Ralph where are you?" his mother says. "Are you all right?"

"I'm fine, mom," Zack replies. "I'm so sorry if I scared you. I'm heading back to the island. I have to work things out with the Constabulary. I'm hoping to see you soon. Can you let Saanvi and Dad know that I'm okay?"

"I will," his mom replies. "Please let me know where you are going to be as soon as you are settled." Zack sees that he has an incoming call from Abby.

"I've got another call I've got to take," Zack says. "I love you, mom."

Zack switches to Abby's call.

"Abby?" Zack says.

Zack hears what he thinks is Abby trying to catch her breath.

"Abby are you okay?"

"I'm frightened RJ," Abby says. "I've never been this frightened in my entire life."

"It's all right now," Zack says, "I think it's all over now."

"When can I see you?" Abby asks.

"I'm still hoping that I can pick you up on Sunday," Zack replies, "but I'm going to have to work that out with the Constabulary."

Zack talks to Abby the entire rest of the ferry ride to the Island. Zack steers clear of saying anything about where he's been, who he has been with and what he has discovered. Zack tells Abby that he realizes that he had made a huge mistake and should not have run off like he did. He spends most of the trip apologizing.

"Listen," Zack replies, "I've got to go meet the Constabulary. I promise that I will call as soon as I am allowed."

"No more wild adventures, RJ," Abby pleads. "Please no more wild adventures."

"No more wild adventures," Zack responds, "I promise."

Zack walks to the gate and gets behind the ten people already in line. He notices that no one is paying any attention to him. When the gates are open, Zack is halfway down the ramp when he sees Phil and another constable standing by the passenger exit. Zack also notes that Molly's Vespa is still parked where he had left it last night.

Zack walks up to Phil, who appears to be scanning the departing passengers for him.

"Looking for someone, officer?" Zack asks.

A Conundrum

Friday, May 9, 10:12AM. Zack is sitting in the front holding cell at the Wannasea Constabulary. He has changed into sweats. Molly's wig and the rest of his disguise has been packed into his backpack. That he is no longer able to roam about freely, tells Zack that the Constabulary is not very happy with him. They've allowed him to use his electronic devices but his trips out of the cell have been limited. The officers in the cell area are not only avoiding him, but they are also refusing to respond to anything which isn't an officially approved request.

Jack Druce comes to his cell with Olivia Stolz in tow. Druce has Zack's cell unlocked but motions for Zack to remain seated on his bunk.

"Glad to see you Olivia," Zack says without a smile.

"Are they treating you properly?' Olivia asks.

"I'm not complaining,' Zack says, "but it is fairly obvious that they aren't very happy with me."

"Should they be?" Olivia asks.

Zack shrugs his shoulders.

"I'm supposed to interview you about your whereabouts after you skipped out from the concert Wednesday night," Druce begins, "but let's skip that until you have a chat with the Captain. I think you may be interested to know that we have arrested Ainsley's cousin and nephew for the Molly Peter's death. The Marines have taken them into custody out at South Island to avoid any more fuss down here. We are working on getting to the bottom of who else at their compound was involved."

"I'm glad to hear that," Zack says. "Do you have any idea why they did it?"

"You are probably one of New Jericho's least favorite people," Druce replies. "We are told Edgar Ainsley has a serious problem with that song which you wrote about him. Ainsley's trial is later in the month. His relatives believed that by creating an act of terror against you, they would somehow be able to negotiate with both the Mainland and the Island to drop the charges against their prophet."

"I don't know if you've paid any attention," Olivia says, "but Ainsley has been making non-stop threats for the past two months to release damning information about anybody, who is anybody over on the Mainland."

"I thought New Jericho was essentially gone when you locked Ainsley up last year," Zack replies.

"Wounded extremist organizations are probably more dangerous than ones which are thriving," Druce replies. "We stop them one place, they pop up in another. We made a mistake by believing New Jericho was declawed with their Prophet gone. We won't make that mistake again."

"Did you guys have any idea that Ainsley's people were behind blowing up my Bug?" Zack asks.

"I can't say that we did specifically, but I'm certain that we'd have gotten there shortly," Druce replies. "By the time that you came back, we had basically determined that the person behind the physical attack on you was not who planted the bomb in your car."

"Do I need to keep worrying about New Jericho?" Zack asks.

"Likely you are never going to be completely in the clear," Jack Druce replies. "As long as you are as popular as you have become, you'll remain a target. It's just a matter of how far New Jericho and people like them are willing to take things."

"Is there any possibility that the same person, who hired someone to rough me up, hired the New Jericho people to plant the explosives?" Zack asks.

Jack Druce studies Zack carefully before replying, "It is not totally out of the realm of possibilities. So far, the only things which we have been able to get out of Ainsley's cousin and nephew is that planting that bomb was a necessary step to bring about God's judgement and that if we do not accept God's judgement, we are doomed to eternal damnation."

"What happens now?" Zack asks.

"You are going to go have a talk with the Captain before that is decided," Jack Druce says. "I'm here to warn you that the Captain is extremely unhappy with you."

"I'm here to let you know," Olivia begins, "that the Constabulary was not within their rights by incarcerating Zack in the first place. Zack may have violated some codes by taking off during the concert, but I am certain that will not stand up in a court of law. However, I've agreed to allow the Captain to speak with you before we determine what comes next."

"Let's go see him," Jack Druce says. "Follow me."

Druce leads Zack and Olivia to a set of offices in the secure area of the administrative section. The Captain's office is the last on the right. Druce walks to the door and knocks lightly.

"Come in," the Captain says.

"Don't feel that you have to agree to anything the Captain offers you," Olivia advises. "I'm certain that I can have you out on bail by tomorrow. It may take us three months, but I'll get whatever charges which may be filled against you dismissed."

Zack walks into the Captain's office.

"Aw Jones," the Captain says pointing to a chair in front of his desk. "Close the door and sit down."

Zack swings the door closed gently then walks to the chair and sits down.

"I think we have what I call a "conundrum"," the Captain says. "You made something of a fool out of the Constabulary by running off like you did Wednesday night, but you also likely saved us a little time by pinpointing Ainsley's people."

Zack remains silent.

"I think we might be able to hold you here for a year if I pressed all of the charges which we feel are applicable," the Captain says. "I'm also aware that may adversely impact the economics of this island. Seems you generate a lot of interest in our Island."

Zack knows when he is being blown smoke by the higher-ups.

"Sir," Zack says, "I'm not sure why it was I was locked up in the first place. I did nothing wrong. I wasn't a suspect."

"We locked you up for your own protection," the Captain replies. "We had the complete right to do that under Island regulations but that's something the lawyers can thrash out."

"What is it exactly that you are thinking of charging me with?" Zack asks.

"I haven't quite decided yet," the Captain says. "I have to weigh the fact that you have greatly embarrassed myself and my men by running off. I've been trying to figure out some way that you can help me avoid that embarrassment. If you can't, we'll simply have to let the lawyers and courts decide."

"I'm sorry sir," Zack says, "but I cannot undo what I did Wednesday night."

"No, you certainly cannot," the Captain says irately. "From what I've been told nobody really knows how you escaped or where you went when you escaped. That is unless you have disclosed your activity to the press or some public person."

"I haven't seen or talked to anyone, who is not part of Constabulary, since I came back to the Island yesterday," Zack replies.

The Captain rubs his hands together and looks off into space for long moments before continuing, "What if I were to tell you that in return for your not disclosing how you went and where you went, I will decide not to bring charges against you?"

"I would agree to that," Zack replies.

"I also want you to know that someone will soon be leaking stories that the Constabulary knew where you were the entire time of your disappearance and in fact had spirited you away themselves," the Captain continues. "This was done to prevent attacks on the Constabulary and to entrap New Jericho. I would expect you to respond to any questions which may be asked about the leaked stories by saying that you have no comment."

"All right," Zack says.

"Then ask Lieutenant Druce to come in and I will see to it that you are discharged at 1PM," the Captain says. "There is a lot of Press outside. We will take you out the back way to avoid questions. Where would you like us to take you?"

"I have a place at Island Resorts," Zack replies. "I'd like to go out there."

Interment

Saturday, May 10, 4:26PM. Zack is standing at the side of Molly's grave site at the Wannasea Cemetery which is located on the west side of the Mountain. He is standing next to his mother and Abe. All of Zack's family including Ray Simmons, 'The Place' staff, former and present, Sam and Dave, the NorthEnders along with a large group of people from the Wannasea Extension are gathered at the gravesite. Standing behind Zack is the ex-Marine bodyguard, who had been at the Villa when Zack had been taken there yesterday afternoon by Constabulary.

Prior to being released from jail, Zack had given Jack Druce a recap of how he left 'The Shell' and what he had done while in Halifax. Zack left out the names of everyone else involved including Mike Papadopoulos. Druce had allowed two uniformed officers to help Zack return Molly's Vespa from the ferry station to her unit at Mountain Village as well as restoring the funds which he had taken from the kitchen drawer. Zack had then been dropped off at Island Resorts.

For the past forty minutes, a group of people from the Wannasea Extension have conducted a ceremony for Molly. They had outlined Molly's time there and continuing involvement with them. Upon completion of their ceremony, Molly's casket was lowered into the grave.

As had been planned earlier in the morning, Beth moves to the front of the grave.

"Molly came to us when she was 17," Beth begins, her voice full of emotion. "We saw her grow from a bright-eyed teenager into a competent young woman. If you are looking for a definition for the term "good girl", Molly was it. An act of unconscionable violence made Molly's life entirely too short. Molly did not deserve an end like this."

With that Beth drops the handful of Wannasea soil which came from the digging of the grave atop Molly's coffin and moves back to standing on the other side of Abe.

Zack walks to the front of the grave. "Molly was my partner," Zack begins. "Molly was there when Zack Tillerman was created. Molly was the biggest driver for Zack Tillerman blossoming. More importantly, Molly became my best friend. Molly never failed to give me good advice. Molly always helped pick me up when I fell. Like many of you here, I have no idea how I am going to be able to go on without her."

Tears streaming down his face, Zack drops his handful of dirt into the grave and returns to his place beside his mother.

Abe goes to the head of the grave.

"Molly was special," Abe says. "As Beth said, Molly was the epitome of a "good girl'. In my life, I have seen too many good people brought down by senseless, selfish acts of violence. I cannot begin to fathom why Molly had to be another of those people. I will now repeat what I have heard much too often at services like these for Molly."

Abe pauses for a second, then recites part of a well-known verse from the "Book of Common Prayer", "We commit this body to the ground; earth to earth, ashes to ashes, dust to dust."

"I shall miss Molly dearly," Abe says as he drops his handful of dirt into Molly's grave. As Abe walks away, most of those in attendance begin placing handfuls of dirt into the gravesite while speaking silent words to themselves.

Zack waits until Melvin Myers, the ex-Marine bodyguard, has placed his handful of dirt.

As they walk to the vehicle, Mel says to Zack, "I really wish that I had been given a chance to know her for more just a few minutes."

Zack places his hand on the bodyguard's arm before saying, "I wish that you had too."

They drive in silence up to 'The Place' whose dining room has been closed for the day. They go inside and participate in the wake until it has ended at 6:30. Zack and the bodyguard then go out to the backstage area of 'The Shell" where Zack changes out of the suit which he had worn to the funeral into the same clothes which he had worn at his first performance at "The Place". Blue jeans, a dark blue shirt and deck shoes without socks.

Beth had talked Zack into going ahead with this night's performance in honor of Molly. All proceeds for the performance will be going to an education fund established at the Extension in Molly's name. For the next hour and half, Zack works with the NorthEnders on plans for the performance.

When 7:30 arrives, Zack begins with the first song which he had recorded, 'Don't Blame it on the Alcohol' and goes through every other song with they have created to 'Dark Thoughts Come'. Zack doesn't take a break. He plays his heart out. When 'Darkness' ends, the lights on the stage come up a little and Zack sets his electric guitar down. Until this moment, Zack had not spoken a word to the audience. When the set began, he and the band had come out, picked up their instruments and began playing. They had not stopped playing until this moment.

"As many of you may know, " Zack begins, "I lost my best pal and business partner, Molly Peters, to utterly senseless violence this past Monday. I'm not really certain how I am going to go on without her. Last year, Molly began playing a song to me called "Wagon Wheel" by Darius Rucker. Although it's a fine song, that style of music isn't my flavor, but I would listen to it with Molly. I found it interesting that she liked Darius Rucker's music so much. If you paid attention to our 'Chadwick and Williams' song tonight, you may have learned a little about my mate, Clint Chadwick. Clint liked Darius Rucker's music as much as Molly. I wished so badly that Clint and Molly had been given the chance to listen to 'Wagon Wheel' together." Zack stops for a moment to collect himself.

"I'm so damned tired of losing my mates to senseless violence," Zack says. "In honor of Molly, we are going to play a modified version of 'Wagon Wheel' for you."

In a lowered voice, Zack says into the microphone, "I hope that Mr. Rucker will forgive us."

After the lights are lowered, the band breaks into the song, everywhere the word "mama" should appear Zack sings "Molly". Tears begin to flow from Zack eyes and drop on to his shirt. Zack makes no attempt to stop the tears or cover them up. When the last stanza of the song is reached, both the band and Zack stop playing their instruments. Zack sings the last stanza without any accompaniment. Then as the band continues to stand silent, Zack, tears still streaming, speaks the last lines of the song which he had just sung,

> "Rock me Molly like a wagon wheel
> rock me Molly anyway you feel
> hey Molly, rock me "

Reunion

Sunday, May 11, 3:04PM. Zack sits in the rear seat of limousine driven by the new bodyguard, who had arrived at the Villa this morning. The vehicle is parked in the parking lot in front of the Coventry Conservatory's Event Center where the bus carrying Abby is due to arrive any second. When they had left for the trip to Coventry for Abby's arrival, the bodyguard informed Zack that he must ride in the rear. Zack had tried unsuccessfully to engage the driver in conversation. The remainder of the trip, Zack spent catching up on messages and trying to figure out not only what he was going to do without Molly but how he is going to deal with the guilt which he feels over Molly's death.

Zack is dressed in the clothes which Abby had bought him to perform two weeks ago. The black jeans are pressed, the silk shirt lightly starched. Zack wears a pair of sunglasses to protect his still slightly black right eye.

Zack is nervous. He badly needs to see Abby but is seriously worried about how this reunion will turn out. It is evident from Abby's messages that she is unhappy that he had disappeared without speaking to her about his plans first. Abby also seems unhappy that Zack remains so vague about what occurred during that disappearance.

Zack sends a message to Alfie explaining the money which he has just sent him to cover the cost of the clothes Babs brought to him and reminding him to tell the others not to breathe a word about what went down on Thursday.

Zack swears to himself that being vague about his activities in Halifax will be the last time that he does not disclose the full truth to Abby. That is assuming that Abby has not already begun moving on from him.

A white bus with red stripes pulls into the parking lot. Zack opens his door and swings out of the limo. He pulls off the sunglasses and hangs them on his belt loop before walking toward the bus. Zack pays no attention to the whispering and pointing as he walks by other waiting people. The bodyguard is on his heels.

Zack stands at the rear of the side door and waits in the sun.

Abby is the third person off the bus. Zack is overwhelmed by how much he has missed her, but based upon the concern displayed on Abby's face, is now less sure how these next few minutes are going to go for him.

Zack begins to fidget like the nervous schoolboy that he had been when he'd first met Abby.

Abby's face holds onto the worry until she steps from the bus and can spot Zack in the bright sunshine. Despite herself, she runs to Zack and wraps her arms around him tighter than she has ever done before.

"Promise me that you will never again disappear to become some sort of out-of-control avenging angel, RJ," Abby says burying her head into the shoulder of Zack's shirt. "I lost you once, I am not going to lose you again."

Zack hugs Abby as tightly as he is able.

"I swear," Zack replies as he kisses Abby's hair, "I won't disappear again unless you ask me to."

"I'm going to hold you to that, RJ," Abby proclaims firmly.

all victims of circumstance
we're victims of circumstance
just more victims of circumstance
more victims of circumstance

For more about books from NG Rippel:

https://www.amazon.com/author/ngrippel

www.ingramcontent.com/pod-product-compliance
Lightning Source LLC
Chambersburg PA
CBHW070508120526
44590CB00013B/780